The Positivity Prescription

A 6-WEEK WELLBEING PROGRAM BASED ON THE SCIENCE OF POSITIVE PSYCHOLOGY

A PROACTIVE APPROACH TO MENTAL HEALTH AND WELLBEING

DR. SUZY GREEN

Australia's leading Positive Psychologist
Founder of The Positivity Institute

First published in 2019 and reprinted in 2025 in Australia by Dr Suzy Green.

P O Box 918, Double Bay, NSW, Australia 1360

Cataloguing-in-Publication entry is available from The National Library of Australia.

www.catalogue.nla.gov.au

ISBN: 978-0-6484890-4-7 (pbk)

Disclaimer: If you have been diagnosed with depression, anxiety or any other psychological disorder, or are concerned about your mental health, please see your General Practitioner before proceeding with the program.

This book is dedicated to my children, Anthea and Sydney, who've inspired me to apply my psychological training to become a better parent and better person. I hope it helps them to realise their potential to be the best version of themselves.

———————————————

I also want to dedicate this book to the hundreds of clients I've worked with and the thousands of students and workshop participants I've been privileged to teach in over 20 years of psychological practice as a clinician, coach and educator.

The knowledge and skills I share in *The Positivity Prescription* I truly believe can and should be taught proactively at school, in the workplace and in our communities.

I hope this book helps create a little more positivity in our world. ✻

"We all want to be happy and live flourishing lives. When you have a positive mindset your cup is full of positivity and you are able to top up other people's cups too. The great news is you can actually learn to be positive. This has been our approach at Starlight and we've experienced inspiring results that have created a positive ripple effect to the children and families we work with. Dr Suzy Green is the maestro of tools and techniques to help anyone become more positive and be their best self. And with positivity being contagious you'll be spreading positivity too."

—Louise Baxter, CEO, The Starlight Children's Foundation

"Insightful and empowering, Dr Suzy Green's book, *The Positivity Prescription*, is a significant contribution to the field of positive psychology. Chock full of processes to live a flourishing life, Suzy's ability to integrate positive psychology and self-leadership is impressive. Highly recommended for anyone wanting to leverage their strengths of character to love the life they live!"

—Fatima Doman, Founder and CEO, Authentic Strengths Advantage™, author of Authentic Strengths and Authentic Resilience

"Dr Suzy Green's personal passion for, and her deep understanding of the science and practice of coaching psychology and positive psychology underpin her global reputation as a key leader in the coaching and positive psychology profession. This book distils over 25 years of her work and gives us a "prescription" for the life well lived. It's evidence-based, it's practical, it's easy to apply to your life – and it works. There's no BS here!"

—Professor Anthony M Grant; Director, Coaching Psychology Unit, University of Sydney

"Average life expectancy in Australia is 82.5 years. Here is a 6-week evidence-based wellbeing program from one of Australia's giants in Positive Psychology - that will make the life you have left so much better for you and the people around you."

—Dr Michael-Carr Gregg, Psychologist, Author, Speaker

"Suzy's wisdom is like chicken soup for the soul. These pages are filled with inspiration, knowledge and guidance to live a richer, more joyful and meaningful life."

—Felicity Harley, Journalist, Author, Founding Editor Women's Health (Australia)

"*The Positivity Prescription* is an easy to follow, inspiring program to help people live their best lives. Not only does Dr Suzy utilise the latest, evidence based strategies within the program but her advice is practical and easy to apply within busy lives. A must read for anyone wanting to create a flourishing, fulfilling life."

—Susie Burrell, Dietitian, Media Personality, Author.

"More than ever, we need to seek guidance from credible sources and from people who are true experts in their field. Dr Suzy is the real deal - decades of experience as both a clinician, keynotes and research. She is one of our nations leaders in the field of wellbeing, happiness and mental health. This book is so timely - filled with scientific based tools and communicated in a clear and relevant way that is for everybody. It will change your life."

—Matt Purcell, Social Media Influencer, Author, Speaker, Host of "The Examined Life" podcast

"*The Positivity Prescription* is written by one of the most experienced and knowledgable experts in clinical, coaching, organisational, and positive psychology. It's a gem of 20 pertinent and practical, science based activities to proactively manage complete mental health – a readable and accessible book for everyone, including friends and family."

—Associate Professor Aaron Jarden, Centre for Positive Psychology, The University of Melbourne

Contents

CONTENTS

Preface

"One can choose to go back toward safety or forward toward growth. Growth must be chosen again and again; fear must be overcome again and again."

ABRAHAM MASLOW

THE POSITIVITY PRESCRIPTION (2ND EDITION)
PREFACE by DR SUZY GREEN

I'm so thrilled to be releasing the second edition of The Positivity Prescription, now with a bonus chapter introducing the seventh **M—Mental Toughness.** Over the years, this book has focused on the proactive enhancement of mental health and wellbeing, offering a framework built around the **6M Model of Flourishing**—*Mood, Motivation, Meaning, Might, Mindfulness, and Mindset.* These six psychological capabilities have been instrumental in enhancing mental health and wellbeing, both for myself, and for the many clients I've worked with over the past 25 years.

With this second edition, I want to take things a step further. While wellbeing remains at the heart of my work, I've increasingly seen the need in today's VUCA (volatile, uncertain, complex and ambiguous) world to explore how these principles support **resilience and mental toughness**—the ability to navigate adversity, maintain focus, and perform at our best under stress, pressure and challenge. In fact, one of the core operating models in my work is the **RAW model,** which stands for *Resilience, Achievement, and Wellbeing* **(see image below)**. It's a framework that highlights the interplay between these key psychological pillars. The science of positive psychology has given us powerful tools to cultivate wellbeing, but it also provides, together with broader psychological theory and research, the skills needed to bounce back from setbacks, stay strong in the face of challenges, and sustain peak performance over time.

In this new edition, you'll find not only the original insights into the 6Ms but also an expanded perspective on how they contribute to resilience and mental toughness. My hope is that as you read, you'll discover practical strategies that you can apply in your own life—whether you're navigating personal struggles, striving for success, or simply looking to strengthen your psychological foundations. These skills have been fundamental to my own mental health and wellbeing and to the many thousands of clients and workshop participants I've supported throughout my career.

I invite you to approach this book as more than just a guide, it's a prescription for thriving in an uncertain world. By integrating the 6Ms with an understanding of mental toughness, I hope you'll find yourself equipped with the mindset and strategies to face life's challenges with greater strength, confidence, and optimism.

Enjoy the journey,

Dr. Suzy Green ✤

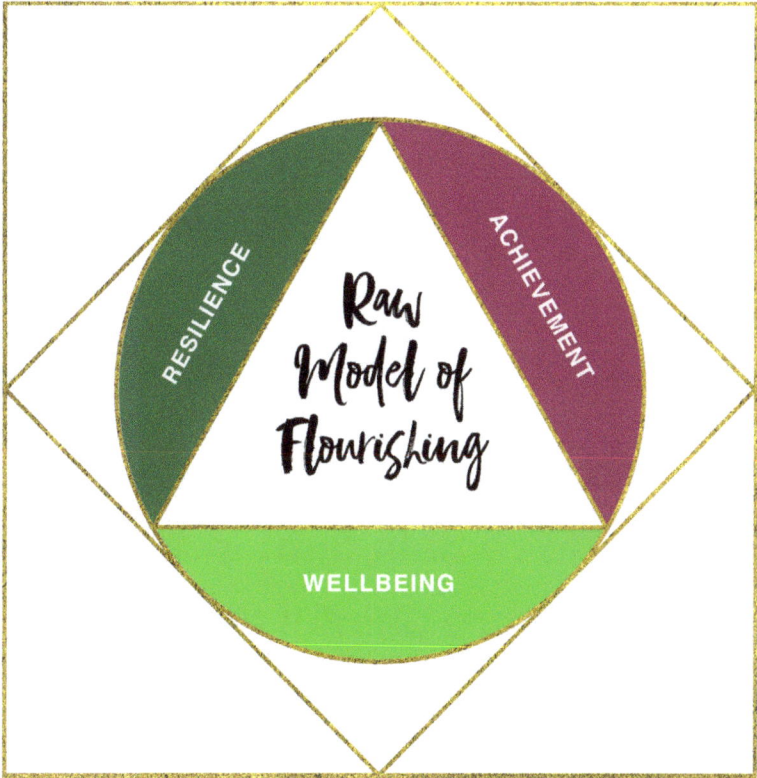

Introduction

"And the day came when the
risk to remain tight in a bud
was more painful than the
risk it took to blossom."

ANAÏS NIN

Well done! By purchasing this book and committing to the six-week program, you've joined an increasing number of people who want to be just as proactive regarding their mental health and wellbeing as they are when it comes to their physical health and wellbeing.

Historically, and currently, the main approach is still reactive — that is, we don't learn the life skills to maintain wellbeing and build resilience until we really need them. These life skills have mainly been taught by Psychologists to their clinical or counselling clients after they've come crashing down or "derailed" and when they are experiencing psychological distress or disorders such as depression and anxiety, which are unfortunately, these days, as common as the common cold!

The Positivity Prescription aims to proactively equip you with the skills to manage the life curve balls and simultaneously boost your mood and create a flourishing life.

Honestly though, how did you feel when you first saw the title of the book? Curious? Cynical? Hopeful? Did you think:

- Is it really possible to create a flourishing life?

- Can I become a more positive person, even if I grew up in a family of pessimists?

- Will this program work for me? I've tried before and failed.

Maybe you're not feeling like your usual self and haven't for a while? You, like many others, may have suffered with depression in the past or you're wondering if you are clinically depressed right now. It might also be a sneaky feeling or a strong knowing you've not reached your potential or achieved your life's dreams and desires and you feel a general sense of dissatisfaction with life? Or perhaps, you were thinking of someone else who might benefit from this book — your husband, wife, partner, parent, grandparent or child?

Or are you a self-help junkie? Someone with a stack of self-help and self-improvement books piled high on your bedside table, but you haven't yet put what you've learned into action. Your self-help books have become "shelf-help" books!

If you've been trying to create positive change for a while now, it may be that you're suffering from what scientists call "willpower fatigue", where you don't have the strength or energy to keep going, stick it out on your own and make the changes you desire. You may have started with good intentions but fallen off the wagon too many times to count.

It doesn't matter which of the above scenarios apply to you, if you're 18 or 80, or if you're not feeling like your best self, then this book is your ready-made roadmap to creating positive change and a flourishing life — where positivity overrides negativity and wellbeing trumps depression. And while *The Positivity Prescription* has been written as a preventative program, its primary focus is on enhancing your wellbeing and helping you to flourish.

The Positivity Prescription is based on the science of Positive Psychology and aims to give you the key psychological skills essential for a flourishing life. That is a life where you're less likely to experience psychological distress and are more likely to experience psychological wellbeing. As you will soon discover, that doesn't mean being happy or positive all the time, but it does mean being confident in your ability to manage the ups and downs of everyday life and to lean into the curve balls when they come. The skills you will learn will also allow you to create meaningful, transformational and sustainable change in your life.

What Is Positive Psychology?

The field of Positive Psychology is a relatively new field of psychology, having been formally launched in 1998 by Professor Martin Seligman, who at the time was the President of the American Psychological Association.

Positive Psychology is defined as the "science of the conditions and processes that lead to optimal human functioning" (Gable & Haidt, 2005). Positive Psychology, though, is an umbrella term for a range of topics relating to the study of optimal human functioning — that is, us at our best. Research has shown that there are over 370 distinct topics that fall under the umbrella of Positive Psychology (Rusk & Waters, 2013). Topics such as wellbeing, character strengths, creativity, grit, love, optimism and meaning to name just a few.

The good news is that after 20 years of scientific research we can reliably identify and prescribe intentional activities scientifically proven to increase our levels of positivity and wellbeing — a true *positivity prescription*.

However, from my own experience and that of my clients, choosing to practice and more importantly continuing to practice these intentional activities is not always easy. In fact, it is challenging for many people. My aim in *The Positivity Prescription* is not only to prescribe proven *Positivity Practices* to boost your mood in the short term but to support you in your lifelong journey in creating and sustaining a flourishing life. Much like the approach we need to take to diet and exercise, it's not like we only need to eat one healthy meal or go to the gym once, there needs to be a lifelong commitment to health and wellbeing — physically and mentally.

Don't be too concerned though, as in concluding the program, we'll proactively address the issue of sustainable changes to help you maintain the positive changes you've implemented along the way.

Positivity: What Is It and Why Do We Need It?

Before we embark on this journey, the most important thing for you to understand is that positivity is NOT about being happy or positive all the time. These days, as the science is becoming more sophisticated, we are realising that happiness is just one aspect of wellbeing and that other human emotions like anger, fear and sadness are also part of wellbeing (you can read more on this in Week 1: Mood).

As a Psychologist, I was trained to help people manage their "negative emotions". I never once had a lecture on happiness, joy or love. Whereas today, 20 years later, a course on "happiness" at Yale received the highest enrolment rate ever — 1,200 students! There's also now a significant amount of research to show that individuals who experience more positive emotions than negative emotions in their daily lives do better in many aspects of life. Numerous studies have shown that happy individuals are successful across multiple life domains, including marriage, friendship, income, work performance and health (Lyubomirsky, King, & Diener, 2005).

Why is happiness linked to successful outcomes? Maybe this research is purely correlative and success in itself creates happiness. While this is true, researchers suggest that it also works the other way. That is, positive moods and emotions lead people to think, feel and act in ways that create success.

Because happy people experience frequent positive moods, they have a greater likelihood of working actively towards new goals while experiencing those moods. Happy people are also in possession of skills and resources, which they have built over time during previous pleasant moods that support them in achieving more success.

All in all, the science supports the proactive enhancement of positive emotions and positivity more broadly. However, it's only recently, with the emergence of Positive Psychology, that we have learned about joy, gratitude, love, optimism and inspiration and how best to cultivate these positive emotions.

I would also argue that it's far easier and better to learn these skills at an early age (which is why Positive Psychology is increasingly taught at schools) and when we are psychologically well rather than distressed, although Positive Psychology can help in many situations.

Overall, there is now undisputable scientific research to attest to the fact that thinking, feeling and behaving more positively leads to a range of beneficial outcomes, including improved psychological and physical health and wellbeing.

The Negativity Bias

Another reason why positivity is so important is that humans have an in-built negativity bias, which is helpful for our survival, but unfortunately also primes us to focus on things that can go wrong. The negativity bias is a psychological phenomenon whereby humans pay more attention to and give more weight to negative rather than positive experiences (Rozin & Royzman, 2001).

There is ample evidence for the existence of the negativity bias. The Scintillating Science box below highlights how science has proven that bad is stronger than good. That's why we need to work extra hard to focus on our strengths and what's working well to help us combat the negativity bias!

Scintillating Science

In a scientific study by Finkenauer and Rimé (1998), researchers asked people to recall a recent, important emotional event that they had either shared with others or kept secret. Although both positive and negative emotional events were welcome and recalled, people reported far more bad events than good events by a four-to-one ratio. The researchers concluded that events involving negative emotions stay on people's minds more than events involving positive emotions. Recall of emotional events appears to favour bad events in that "bad is stronger than good".

An Uncertain World

We're living in a VUCA (volatile, uncertain, complex and ambiguous) world. There's never been a time in history when the pace and rate of change have been so fast. Sitting with uncertainty is not easy for a species that's primed for survival and safety. We also have the most incredible opportunities available to us for the first time ever. Due to technology, we can access information that took years to learn previously and we can connect with people from all over the globe that we never would have met.

All in all, this is positive, however the options available to us can sometimes feel overwhelming and we don't know which path to take. Sometimes our best plans change and we need to regroup fast. We also need to be able to help our families and friends adapt to this uncertain world.

Our parents and grandparents typically led linear lives. That is, they usually had one job or career for life, one marriage, children if they were fortunate, retirement and then death. Our own lives are more cyclical. That is, we tend to cycle through life stages. And whilst the cycles can bring some form of certainty, with change the new normal, we need to be ready to change course rapidly. This requires agility, what's known as psychological flexibility.

The Positivity Prescription aims to equip you with the key psychological skills to build agility, flexibility and allow you to thrive, not just survive, in this uncertain world.

That's why I strongly believe we can and should be teaching these skills in our schools, workplaces and communities. We can't continue to be reactive, knowing that the only certainties in life are death, taxes and change! That's why I wrote *The Positivity Prescription*.

My Positivity Journey

The Positivity Prescription is not just a book based on science written by an academic. It is a culmination of my life journey so far as a practitioner and as a person. I have been wanting to write this book for over 10 years, but instead ended up writing over 20 academic book Modules and scientific journal articles. A great accomplishment, you might think? Well yes, but the truth is, no one reads them. At least, not the people I want to influence most — people like you.

I have worked hard at creating a flourishing life. I have personally tested every technique in this book and I can honestly tell you that while I haven't achieved all my life goals (yet) and my life is certainly not perfect, it is pretty damn good — I am currently flourishing!

Whilst I've personally benefited from my studies and career in psychology and also helped my clients benefit over the years, I wanted to share this information more broadly with the wider community. I'm passionate about proactivity and enabling people to make positive changes in their lives. I am a huge fan of *The Biggest Loser* and any type of program where people enact and more importantly sustain positive change.

Professionally, I've studied human behaviour, mental health and wellbeing for nearly 30 years. I hold a Doctorate in Clinical Psychology (I understand what it means to be mentally ill) and I also conducted a world-first study on evidence-based life coaching (Green, Oades, & Grant, 2006) as a mental health prevention and promotion intervention. I also taught Applied Positive Psychology at the University of Sydney for 10 years.

I've spent the past 20 years as a Clinical and Coaching Psychologist, working with over 500 clients to improve not only their psychological wellbeing, but their lives. I have seen amazing success stories and been privileged to sit with people through the discomfort, anxiety and failures that so often accompany deep change.

Early on in my career, my first job was as an Intern Psychologist in a private psychiatric clinic. At the time, I had no idea that the clients I consulted with would be the most distressed and challenged clients I would ever work with in my career. Many of them had suffered significant traumas and horrendous family upbringings and had developed serious psychological disorders.

In these early days, I had two major light-bulb moments. The first one was that I couldn't do this type of work all day, every day, for the rest of my life. After seeing client after client (some days I saw eight clients back-to-back, without a lunch break), I felt completely drained and my mood started to suffer.

I usually had a very robust, cheerful mood, which was an asset for my work, but I could see that it wouldn't take too long before my own mental health would deteriorate. I had to face the fact that I may not be able to continue doing the work I loved.

The second light-bulb moment was that I realised that it was crazy that practitioners waited until people came crashing down with depression or anxiety before giving them the knowledge and skills to cope. I started to wonder why I hadn't learned these skills at school and why my children (aged 9 and 12 then) weren't learning these skills at school either.

At this time, I was in the midst of a divorce, with two small children to care for. I had, like most people who go through divorce, found it the most challenging experience in my life so far. I realised that I too had been and was continuing to experience some psychological distress. Nothing like that of my clients, but primarily in the form of stress and anxiety.

I realised that the knowledge and skills I had learned in my psychology studies were not just interesting theories but life-changing tools that not only were benefitting my clients, but could also help me get through this challenge.

For the last 20 years, I have continued to study optimal human functioning and teach the science to others. I have also been privileged to be part of a group of people who have witnessed and been part of a major shift in the science of psychology, from a focus on deficits to a focus on strengths and from a focus on illness prevention to promoting wellbeing.

My mission now is to share this life-changing information with the wider world: schools, workplaces and communities. I spend most of my time giving keynote presentations and workshops about the information contained in this book. The emergence of the field of Positive Psychology and its increasing media coverage and popularity in the community leads me to speak to very diverse audiences including lawyers, engineers, disability workers, nurses and teachers. Most people want to lead a happy and healthy life and they understand that the science underpinning Positive Psychology can help them achieve that.

Having spoken on the topic of Positive Psychology for so long now, I realised the time had come to put this information down in a self-coaching format so that people can apply it to improve their lives without engaging a professional (although that can be helpful or necessary at times).

High Hopes

Are you feeling more hopeful about what the program can offer you? As you'll soon discover, hope isn't just a "thing with feathers on it", as Emily Dickinson once said. It is a well-validated psychological theory that can be applied to support you in achieving your goals and enhancing your wellbeing (you can read more about hope theory in Week 2: Motivation).

I'd like to share my hopes for you before we begin our journey, even though I will be here cheering you on the whole way. My biggest hope for you is that you will not only read this book but apply its teachings to transform your life. False promises, you're thinking? Well no, remember, all the information and recommendations in this book are based on scientific research.

As a clinician and coach, I have tested every technique with dozens of clients and on myself. I know it works, although different people might require different techniques. It is about being open to new experiences and showing a willingness to experiment even if your first thoughts are "This won't work for me". Be prepared to be pleasantly surprised!

While the techniques I will share with you may not prevent everyone from developing depression or other mental illnesses, I live in hope that it may prevent many instances of them. While I believe this book will definitely help combat the growing incidence of mental illness, my biggest hope is that it will help people like you live flourishing lives filled with more positivity, joy and love.

And please don't think this is indulgent or selfish. Recent science on the social and emotional contagion effect tells us that when you flourish, others will too. In short, our positivity (similarly to our negativity) is contagious. I hope that those who read and complete *The Positivity Prescription* create a positive contagion effect, creating a more flourishing world. This means you can help create a world where more people flourish and are filled with joy, compassion and love.

About the Program

The Positivity Prescription is a six-week program based on the science of Positive Psychology that is designed to improve your positivity and general wellbeing. I know from personal experience and in working with hundreds of clients that if you commit to the program in an open and heart-felt way and schedule the time to read, reflect and use the recommended *Positivity Practices*, then this program can transform your life.

The Positivity Prescription is based on six core elements of wellbeing and peak performance found to be essential in increasing levels of positivity, reducing distress and creating a flourishing life. These six elements are mood, motivation, might, meaning, mindfulness and mindset, which we will cover in depth during the program.

There is a systematic approach to the six-week program, so it is best to start at the beginning and read each Module in turn. You might like to start on a Monday or possibly on the first day of the month to give you the feeling that this is a new beginning for you. You might also find that there's a lot to take in and that you want to take a fortnight to complete each Module. That's fine too. It's about experimenting with what works for you.

This introduction Module and the concluding Module will help you make the most out of the program and sustain the positive changes you have made, even after the program is over. Here's a snapshot of the six-week program.

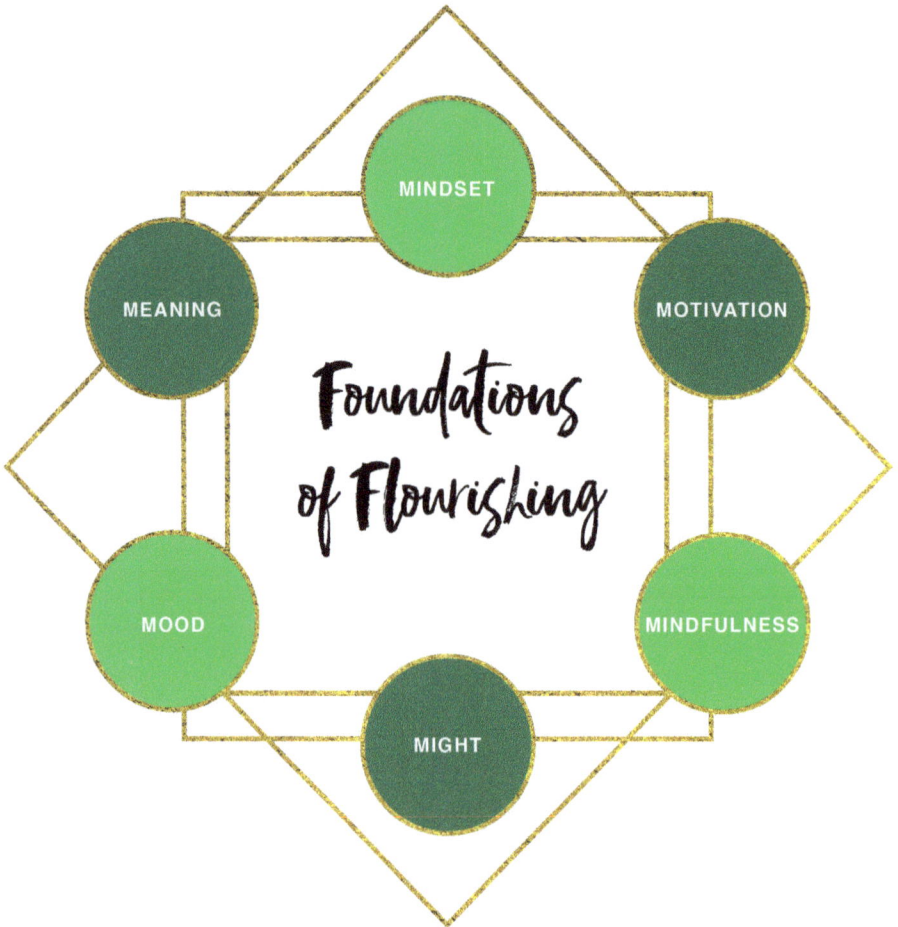

Foundations of Flourishing

MINDSET
MEANING
MOTIVATION
MOOD
MINDFULNESS
MIGHT

Week 1: Mood

Week 1 introduces you to moods and emotions with a specific focus on positive emotions. This includes scientific strategies proven to boost your mood.

Week 2: Motivation

In week 2, we work towards increasing your motivation for change by understanding your readiness and reasons for change. This includes a values assessment and a visioning exercise.

Week 3: Might

Week 3 introduces you to the concept of character strengths and their powerful effects on goal achievement and wellbeing. We'll also learn about lesser strengths and why their development is important.

Week 4: Meaning

Week 4 will help you identify your authentic desires and transform them into meaningful life goals. We will also use job-crafting activities to create more meaningful work for you.

Week 5: Mindfulness

Week 5 introduces you to the concept of mindfulness as a non-negotiable strategy for wellbeing. A range of strategies are provided to help you increase your levels of mindfulness.

Week 6: Mindset

Week 6 will help you identify automatic negative thoughts that undermine your wellbeing. You will have an opportunity to create performance-enhancing thoughts to supercharge your wellbeing and achievement.

Positivity Practices

Over the course of the program, I will be sharing with you 20 Positive Psychology practices that have been scientifically tried and tested. I will also encourage you to take up weekly challenges where you'll put your knowledge into action. Yes, you are going to have to put in some work! The weekly challenge involves trialling and testing the *Positivity Practices* that are scientifically proven to improve psychological wellbeing and reduce the symptoms of depression. Some of these practices will be a one-off exercise during the program and others will become part of your daily routine.

When I taught Applied Positive Psychology at the University of Sydney, testing the *Positivity Practices* on yourself was an assessable component of the course. Most of the students started off doing practices like mindfulness, strength spotting and gratitude because they felt they had to, but after a while they began to report on the powerful positive impacts these interventions were having. My students knew they were flourishing — and their family and friends started to notice the change! Eventually, with such positive reinforcement, the techniques became part of their lives and who they were becoming — much more mindful and grateful people.

So, try not to be cynical of these challenges and give them a try!

Success Stories

Throughout the book I'll be sharing stories and examples of past students, clients and workshop participants to bring the science to life and highlight the benefits of the *Positivity Practices*. Of course, as a Psychologist, it's important to maintain confidentiality, so all stories and examples will be a fictitious combination of my real-life experience in teaching the skills contained in the book. My hope is that hearing and relating to these personal stories will help you consider how the practices may work for you.

While the focus is definitely on highlighting success to give you hope and motivation, you'll also need to be prepared for discomfort and challenges, particularly if the practice is something you've never tried before or if it doesn't feel like something you would normally do.

By reading the stories of success, you'll learn some great tips for troubleshooting. You'll also realise that the challenges you're experiencing are not just peculiar to you but that they're a normal part of the process. If you understand that, you're less likely to give up and more likely to have another go if the *Positivity Practice* doesn't have the impact you were looking for the first time round.

Get a Journal

I highly recommend you purchase a dedicated journal to record your thoughts and impressions as you complete *The Positivity Prescription*. In fact, I'm going to recommend that you keep the book and journal together on your bedside table or wherever else you read. That way, the journal is handy for you to make notes as you read. I'll also be asking reflective questions throughout the book, so the journal makes for a great place to keep all of this information together for you to review and re-read. Overall, the journal together with what you're learning in *The Positivity Prescription* will help you to gain greater levels of self-awareness as you progress through the book.

For those who still might find the idea of journalling a little New Age or infantile, you might like to know that there is a significant amount of research on therapeutic journalling. People who express their thoughts and emotions through writing can experience huge wellbeing benefits.

We have some of our own beautiful positivity journals (www.thepositivityinstitute. com.au/product/positivity-journal/), but there are many other beautiful journals on the market. Be sure to pick one that you love and will want to use — that's key to journalling success!

Get a Coach

While I am hoping the book itself will help keep you motivated and on track, it's also going to be helpful to identify a coach to support you along the way. This coach could be a professional coach, a colleague or a buddy who will support you in implementing the program over the six weeks. You can even enlist them in the program with you! And if it's not too spooky for you, you can also think of me as your own personal virtual coach, a Jiminy Cricket if you like, who sits on your shoulder, cheering you on to success and helping you to reflect and act on the *Positivity Practices*.

So, are you ready to get started? ❖

What *The Positivity Prescription* is not

A magic bullet. Research from neuroscience tells us that behavioural change requires neural change in our brains and neural change requires practice. Generally, change won't be automated until around the two-month mark.

It's not about being happy all the time. It's about experiencing the full range of human emotions. If you have difficulty with negative emotions like anger, fear and sadness, it's important to seek professional help.

It's not about thinking positively. It's not a New Age idea that if we "think positive" we can create, in an instant, the body we've always wanted or the partner of our dreams! *The Positivity Prescription* is about thinking in ways that support our goals rather than hinder them.

A fad. In the field of physical health and nutrition, science has consistently updated our knowledge despite contradictory studies and confusion. Because of that, most of us now know the foundations of good physical health. Similarly, we also know the foundations of good mental health. This program is about establishing those foundations and, of course, encouraging you to work on your positive health more broadly.

A panacea. Whilst the program is based on science and the *Positivity Practices* have been shown to be effective, it's important to note that not all practices will reap the same benefits for everyone and that the program won't necessarily fix everything in your life. It's about taking the knowledge and applying it to life's challenges and continually testing and trialling.

Week 1: Mood

"One joy dispels a hundred cares."

CONFUCIUS

Welcome to Week 1: Mood, in which we'll explore whether you're flourishing or languishing. Our first module will also help you understand what positivity is and what we're aiming for and why.

_____

This week, we will be taking a closer look at:

- Moods and emotions, and the difference between them.

- Whether you are flourishing or languishing.

- The role of positivity in creating a flourishing life.

- Mood-boosting strategies proven by science.

Before we begin, and for every week of the program, I would like you to grab your journal and pen to record any light-bulb moments or personal insights.

Emotions and Moods

Do you know the difference between emotions and moods? Most people do not. Generally, our knowledge of emotions as a community is pretty limited, with most people having restricted emotional vocabularies and a low level of skills to manage their emotions, particularly the problematic ones like sadness and anger.

Emotions are our feelings. They create changes in our bodies, our physiology, our thoughts and our behaviours. For example, when you feel the emotion of excitement, you experience butterflies in your stomach and you have a desire to move towards the exciting activity rather than away from it. Compare this to fear, where you feel your heart racing and your palms sweating, and you want to move away from the feared person or situation. It's important to recognise that emotions are not necessarily good or bad, they simply provide us with important information for our survival, both in the short and long term.

In comparison, a mood is an emotional state. We generally describe our moods as good or bad. A mood may last a while, a few days often, whereas emotions are fleeting and can shift quickly from one to another. We can move from feelings of hurt to anger so quickly that we don't even realise that we are feeling hurt and lash out in anger.

In the introduction Module, we learned about positivity. We learned that this program is not about helping you be happy or positive all the time. It is about helping you to flourish.

The term flourishing is used commonly in the science of Positive Psychology and you've heard it numerous times now in reading this book, but what does it mean to you and me, in terms of our wellbeing and daily lives?

Flourishing or Languishing?

Fortunately, a lot of research has gone into helping us understand what it means to flourish. In the 1960s, the famous Psychologist Professor Abraham Maslow spoke about "self-actualisation" as a form of optimal human development. The Oxford English Dictionary defines self-actualisation as "the realisation or fulfilment of one's talents and potentialities, especially considered as a drive or need present in everyone". Professor Carl Rogers, another well-known Psychologist of the time, referred to the "fully functioning individual", someone who is in touch with his or her deepest and innermost feelings and desires. These individuals understand their emotions and place a deep trust in their own instincts and urges.

Rogers also suggested that people have an actualising tendency and a need to achieve their full potential, similar to Maslow's "self-actualisation". Rogers believed that a fully functioning person is continually working towards becoming self-actualised. This individual receives unconditional positive regard from others, does not place conditions on his or her own worth, is capable of expressing feelings and is fully open to life's experiences.

Today, in the field of Positive Psychology, we are still focused on being our best selves and self-actualising, however there's a stronger usage of the language relating to wellbeing or flourishing, the term used more commonly these days. The focus on wellbeing is primarily due to the rising incidence of mental illness in our communities and the recognition that we need to proactively build wellbeing and simultaneously reduce mental illness.

I personally believe that somewhere along the wellbeing journey, or the rise of Positive Psychology, we've lost sight of the original purpose of Positive Psychology. That is, to understand the conditions and processes of optimal human functioning. More recently though, there's been a resurgence of interest in self-actualisation, spear-headed by the scholar Dr Scott Barry Kaufman. You can read more about Scott's work on human potential on his website (scottbarrykaufman.com/).

Positive Psychology sits on the shoulders of Humanistic Psychology and we have a lot to thank Maslow and Rogers for. Thanks to a more contemporary and sophisticated approach to research and design in Positive Psychology, we now have a really good sense of what it is to flourish (or languish as the case may be) and how well we are doing as a society in this regard.

You will be pleased to know that research has shown that most of us (approximately 50%) are moderately mentally healthy. While that's not bad, I often wonder who wants to just be moderately mentally healthy — particularly when we're not on the planet for a long time. The not so great news is that only a few us (approximately 20%) are flourishing and report high levels of psychological wellbeing. The rest of us are either diagnosed as clinically depressed or languishing (i.e. reporting low levels of psychological wellbeing; Keyes, 2007; Huppert, 2005).

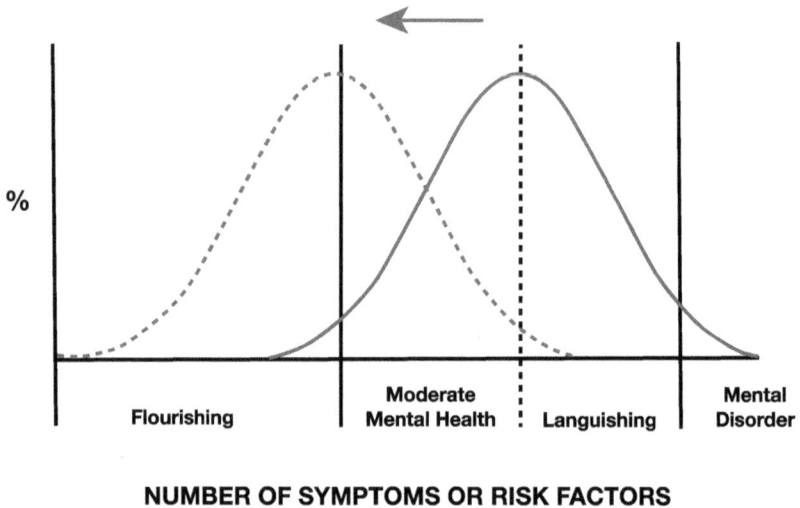

NUMBER OF SYMPTOMS OR RISK FACTORS

In Positive Psychology, to flourish is defined as "to live within an optimal range of human functioning, one that connotes goodness, generativity, growth and resilience" (Fredrickson & Losada, 2005). Flourishing is the opposite of pathology and languishing, which are described as living a life that feels hollow and empty.

However, research has shown that if we only treat those with mental disorders, these actions will not be sufficient to shift the population bell curve towards a more flourishing state. Whilst there's definitely a need for treatment as the alarming statistics suggest, we simultaneously need proactive, non-stigmatised Positive Psychology programs for those who are languishing or in the "moderately mentally healthy" categories to move more people towards flourishing. That's the reason I created *The Positivity Prescription*.

Are You Flourishing?

The flourishing scale was developed by Dr Robert Biswas-Diener and Professor Ed Diener, pioneers in the study of happiness and wellbeing. While there are no set categories in terms of a certain low score indicating you are a languisher or a certain high score indicating you are a flourisher, I have included the scale to help you determine whether this book is right for you to proceed with at this time.

While this scale is not meant to diagnose depression, anxiety or any other disorder, if your scores are low across many of the questions, this may be indicative of distress or disorder and I would recommend you consult with your General Practitioner as soon as possible. You can also undertake a depression self-assessment on the Black Dog Institute website (www.blackdoginstitute. org.au/resources-support/digital-tools-apps/depression-self-test/). If you would like to access a list of mental health services and resources, please refer to the back of this book.

If in completing this scale, you believe you are clinically depressed, anxious or suffering from another psychological disorder, I recommend you seek help quickly. We have many evidence-based psychological interventions that can successfully treat psychological distress and disorder, so do not put it off any longer!

We need to lose the stigma of seeking help. Here in Australia, we are a long way from New York, where people brag about having a therapist. Many people falsely think that seeing a shrink means lying on a couch for years, unearthing and sharing deep, dark secrets from your childhood. While that may be true in some instances, for most people, only 6 to 12 sessions of therapy are necessary.

Many of my clients have said that having therapy changed their life. They wondered why they did not do this earlier on in life. It is far easier to boost our wellbeing when we are doing not too bad. It is much harder to boost your wellbeing and undertake this program if you are depressed or anxious.

The Flourishing Scale

© Copyright by Professor Ed Diener and Dr Robert Biswas-Diener, January 2009

Below are eight statements with which you may agree or disagree. Using the one to seven scale below, indicate your agreement with each item.

7 — Strongly agree
6 — Agree
5 — Slightly agree
4 — Neither agree nor disagree
3 — Slightly disagree
2 — Disagree
1 — Strongly disagree

_____ I lead a purposeful and meaningful life.
_____ My social relationships are supportive and rewarding.
_____ I am engaged and interested in daily activities.
_____ I actively contribute to the happiness and wellbeing of others.
_____ I am competent and capable in the activities that are important to me.
_____ I am a good person and live a good life.
_____ I am optimistic about my future.
_____ People respect me.

Scoring: Add your responses scores, varying from one to seven, for all eight items. Possible scores range from 8 (lowest possible) to 56 (highest possible). A high score represents a person with many psychological resources and strengths. Please note your personal reflections in your journal now.

Source: Diener, E., Wirtz, D., Tov, W., Kim-Prieto, C., Choi, D., Oishi, S., & Biswas-Diener, R. (2009). New measures of well-being: Flourishing and positive and negative feelings. Social Indicators Research, 39, 247-266.

Success Story

Susan came for life coaching stating she hadn't been feeling her usual self lately, although she certainly didn't feel like she needed counselling or major therapy. She had undertaken therapy previously and had found it to be very helpful. She said her goals were to be happier, more content with what life had given her and to rediscover her life purpose.

Susan completed the Flourishing Scale and calculated a score of 40 out of 56. In completing the scale, she realised that there was actually more going right for her than she realised. She had many positive relationships with family and friends and was involved in activities she loved, like her weekly tennis lesson and dance class. She was surprised to see that her score in regard to optimism was lower than expected. So too were her self-reported levels of competency and capability. She wasn't surprised to see that her score in regard to leading a meaningful life was also low.

The insights she gained were used to help Susan clarify her coaching goals, which related to improving her mood. She decided to focus on: building optimism (see Week 6: Mindset) and hope (see Week 2: Motivation) and increasing meaning (see Week 4: Meaning).

The Positivity Ratio

If you have done any reading on Positive Psychology, you may have come across something referred to as the positivity ratio, a term originally coined by Professor Barbara Fredrickson and Professor Marcial Losada. This ratio was initially identified as being 3:1. That is, to flourish, you needed to experience three positive emotions to every negative emotion.

In recent years, the mathematical formulation for the positivity ratio has been critiqued and the ratio no longer stands as valid. However, that doesn't mean we should throw the baby out with the bathwater! It makes common sense that a flourishing individual or someone with high levels of wellbeing and low levels of mental illness is going to experience more positive emotions than negative emotions daily.

Let's take a further look at what this means in terms of creating a flourishing life. For individuals, to flourish means to experience higher levels of positive emotions (i.e. love, joy and gratitude) compared to negative emotions (i.e. sadness and anger) in daily life. We know that someone with clinical depression or someone who is languishing experiences the opposite, feeling a larger amount of daily negative emotions, with little positivity.

When it comes to our relationships, to flourish means to experience a higher ratio of positive behaviours and interactions, such as support, encouragement and love, compared to negative behaviours and interactions, such as cynicism, sarcasm and negativity.

In his ground-breaking research on marriages, Dr John Gottman (also known as Dr Love) identified a scientifically proven ratio of 5:1 for "master marriages" versus "disaster marriages", which sit at around 0.8:1. This means that for every negative comment or behaviour, five positive ones are needed to combat it. You might like to share this information with your loved one!

Primed for Positivity

There is a natural phenomenon known as heliotropism, whereby plants lean towards the light (you might have observed it in sunflowers). This natural tendency exists in every living system (including humans) whereby we move towards what is life giving and energising (the light) and we move away from negative and draining energy (the dark). It is hypothesised that this tendency is for pure survival. That is, we are primed to create energy needed for our survival.

Despite research that supports the concept of the negativity bias as we've already learned, there is also research to support that we are also simultaneously primed for positivity. Humans can't always focus on potential negatives or else they would never go anywhere to explore new environments in search of potential rewards. Research suggests that in new or unfamiliar territory, when rewards are not yet learned, there might instead be a positivity bias to help push people towards exploration (Sparks & Ledgerwood, 2017).

Research in support of this notion shows that people remember and learn positive information faster and more accurately than negative information, positive words predominate over negative words in all languages and human brains are more activated by positivity than by negativity.

Sparks and Ledgerwood (2017) suggest that we may integrate these two somewhat contradictory bodies of research by understanding that humans may have evolved a cognitive architecture that not only helps them avoid potential negatives (i.e. losses) but also pushes them to explore novel or foreign environments in search of potential rewards (i.e. gains; Cacioppo et al., 1997; Fazio et al., 2004).

Professor Kim Cameron also suggests that when it comes to organisations, leaders that capitalise on the positive tend to produce life-giving, flourishing outcomes. A focus on the positive is life giving for individuals and organisations in the same way that positive energy in nature encourages living organisms to thrive.

Scintillating Science

In 1930, 180 nuns in their early twenties wrote brief autobiographies. Each nun was asked by her Mother Superior to write a short sketch of her life. The essay was to contain no more than two to three hundred words on a single sheet of paper. The nuns were asked to include place of birth, parentage, interesting childhood events, schools, influences that led to the convent, religious life and outstanding events. Over 70 years later, in 2001, their words predicted their lifespan.

In this famous study often referred to as the "nun study" (Danner, Snowdon, & Friesen, 2001), researchers analysed the nuns' letters for positive emotional content and related the content to the nuns' survival between the ages of 75 and 95.

The study revealed that the nuns whose autobiographies contained the most sentences expressing positive emotions lived an average of seven years longer than nuns whose stories contained the fewest. Lifespan increased by nine years for nuns whose autobiographies contained the most words referring to positive emotions and by ten years for nuns who used the greatest variety of words describing positive emotions.

Can You Be Too Positive?

Yes, you can! Research has shown that there can be issues with being too positive or overly optimistic. Whilst optimism is generally something to be cultivated and you'll be reading more about that in Week 6: Mindset, overplayed optimism can be detrimental.

Optimism bias is defined as the tendency for people to be overly optimistic about certain outcomes, for example, overestimating the likelihood of positive events (such as winning the lottery) and underestimating the likelihood of negative events (such as being a victim of crime).

Excessive or delusional optimism can result in making poor decisions and delays when plans are implemented or expensive projects are built. This is often referred to as the planning fallacy. This is where we underestimate how long it will take to complete a task or project or hold a meeting. The planning fallacy was first proposed by Professor Daniel Kahneman and Dr Amos Tversky in 1979. In extreme cases, this delusional optimism leads to poor decisions that can result in project failures, market crashes and even defeats in military conflicts (Flyvbjerg, Garbuio, & Lovallo, 2009).

While thinking positively about ourselves is generally beneficial for us, research has shown that this is not always the case. Positive self-statements (or affirmations) are widely believed to boost mood and self-esteem, yet a scientific study showed that when participants with low self-esteem repeated a positive self-statement (e.g. "I'm a lovable person"), they tended to feel worse than those who did not repeat the statement. The participants with high self-esteem felt better when they repeated the statement, but to a limited degree. The researchers concluded that repeating positive self-statements can benefit certain people but can also backfire for the very people who need them the most (Wood, Perunovic, & Lee, 2009).

The researchers hypothesised that when there's a discrepancy between how we feel about ourselves and what we're telling ourselves is our ideal state, the greater the discrepancy, the worse we'll feel. The positive self-statement seems to highlight the deficiency between how we are now and how we'd like to be. So, if you repeat the statement, "I am a lovable person" and you say to yourself (consciously or not), "But I know I'm not as lovable as I could be, or as lovable as Jane ..." then you're less likely to believe the affirmation. That is, if we hold negative self-views about ourselves, we may resist information about ourselves that is overly positive (Swann Jr & Schroeder, 1995).

The Power of Positive Emotions

Thankfully, there is growing recognition that positivity is much more than a "big, happy, smiling face". Growing research from Positive Psychology is continuing to support the notion that increased positive emotions such as gratitude, joy, interest, hope, inspiration and love do more than just make us feel good.

Research based on the Broaden and Build Theory shows that positivity broadens our minds and expands our range of vision. The Broaden and Build Theory (Fredrickson, 1998, 2001) asserts that positive emotions evolved as psychological adaptations that increased our ancestors' odds of survival and reproduction. While negative emotions narrow people's behavioural urges towards specific actions (i.e. fight, flight or freeze), positive emotions widen our array of thoughts and actions. The benefits of broadened mindsets build a variety of personal resources such as social connections, coping strategies and environmental knowledge, reserves we can later draw on to manage threats. Therefore, the cultivation of positive emotions is essential for our mental health, wellbeing and survival. Another key benefit of a broadened mindset is increased creativity. Given the competitive environments we live in today, high levels of creativity and innovation are essential for success.

Professor Barbara Fredrickson, a leader in the study of positive emotions, has identified ten major positive emotions:

| Gratitude | Interest | Pride | Inspiration | Love |
| 2 | 4 | 6 | 8 | 10 |

| 1 | 3 | 5 | 7 | 9 |
| Joy | Serenity | Hope | Amusement | Awe |

Prioritising Positivity

Cross-cultural research supports the fact that everyone wants to be happy. As you've just read, experiencing positive emotions not only helps us feel good, it affects how we function.

But did you know that research has shown that the obsessive pursuit of happiness has the opposite effect and in fact can make you feel worse? Research has shown that rather than overvaluing happiness and potentially feeling worse, prioritising positivity on a daily basis might be the key to wellbeing (Catalino, Algoe, & Fredrickson, 2014). Prioritising positivity means designing and/or organising your daily life to maximise the experience of positive emotions. Research has shown that people who put themselves in situations or contexts where they are likely to experience a range of positive emotions are more likely to feel happier and experience fewer depressive symptoms. Another form of prioritising positivity is known as "pleasant event scheduling", such as playing with pets. This is a key strategy prescribed for the treatment of clinical depression.

Reflect on the questions to consider how actively you currently prioritise positivity in your life. There's no scoring here as the aim is to raise your awareness of your current approach to creating positivity and happiness in your life.

How Much Do You Currently Prioritise Positivity?

Answer with a yes or no.

- One of my priorities is experiencing happiness in everyday life.

- I look for and nurture my positive emotions.

- What I decide to do with my time outside of work is influenced by how much I might experience positive emotions.

- I structure my day to maximise my happiness.

- My major decisions in life are influenced by how much I might experience positive emotions.

- I admire people who make decisions based on the happiness they will gain.

It's important to note that the activities you choose to create positive emotions in your life may differ significantly from those chosen by others. One person may choose to reserve Saturday afternoon for their families, yet another may choose to dedicate it to their own pleasurable pursuits. Some people will want to experience activities that create a sense of calm and contentment whereas others may want to experience excitement and energy.

Which of the ten positive emotions identified by Professor Fredrickson do you want to feel more of? Pause now and jot down in your journal any thoughts or ideas you have about the emotions you want to feel and how best to create them in your daily life.

Mood-Boosting Strategies Supported by Science

Two main factors play a role in the enhancement and maintenance of positive emotions. The first one is that strategies must be performed with effort and habitual commitment. This can be done through prioritising positivity, as you've discovered. The second is the importance of a strategy that fits with a person's personality, motives, strengths and needs. This means that for the strategies to work, we need to be prepared to stick at them for a while and be willing to assess whether they're a good fit for us.

Sometimes, it's too easy to write off a strategy too quickly, thinking it won't work for me. I have seen time and time again people pleasantly surprised that some strategies are more powerful than they could ever have anticipated! This is why it is so important to cultivate a mindset of curiosity and a willingness to experiment to make the most of this program.

However, it's also important to recognise that some strategies won't be the best fit for us and that's okay too.

Let's take a closer look at specific strategies that have been scientifically proven to increase positivity and psychological wellbeing. These include, but are not limited to:

- Increasing hope and optimism.

- Practising acts of kindness (random or intentional).

- Nurturing positive relationships at work and in our personal lives.

- Savouring and reminiscing on life's joys.

- Setting and striving for personally meaningful goals.

- Learning to forgive and let go of grudges.

- Regular physical exercise.

- Cultivating and expressing gratitude.

Some of these strategies are self-explanatory. If you would like to learn more about these activities, I recommend you read *The How of Happiness* by Professor Sonja Lyubomirsky. While my aim is to give you every strategy that will support your success, unfortunately, I will not be able to explore all these mood-boosting strategies in detail.

As part of this week's homework, I will ask you to trial three strategies that have been shown to have a powerful effect on wellbeing. These are gratitude, kindness and forgiveness.

Gratitude

Gratitude is one of the most researched areas of Positive Psychology and a significant number of studies have found that people who feel more gratitude experience more positive emotions, experience less anger, are more optimistic, have more positive relationships, sleep better and have lower levels of depression (Emmons & McCullough, 2003).

Cultivating gratitude is about appreciating what you have rather than focusing on what you don't. It's hypothesised that one of the primary reasons why gratitude is so powerful is that it prevents us from taking things for granted. Proactively counting your blessings can significantly boost your mood in less than a month (Emmons & McCullough, 2003). Researchers have also demonstrated that grateful individuals are especially appreciative of the contribution of others to their happiness (McCullough et al., 2001). Compared with unhappy people, happy people report close and satisfying relationships and feel more gratitude in their lives (Park, Peterson, & Seligman, 2004). There is also a close connection between kindness and gratitude, whereby gratitude is experienced when people receive kindness from other people.

Positivity Practice #1: Count Your Blessings

There are many things in our lives, both large and small, to be grateful for. In this practice, I want you to count your blessings every night this week before bed (or three times at least). Use your journal or an app to reflect on the day. Write down up to five things you are grateful for or have a sense of appreciation for. That might be as simple as your health, your friends and family, or a smooth ride to work that day. You might also like to do the exercise now as a warm up.

You might like to share your list with your family and friends. Many families I've worked with make this a regular practice at evening mealtimes around the dinner table. While we don't celebrate Thanksgiving here in Australia, why not think about making this ritual an everyday activity rather than once a year?

1. _____

2. _____

3. _____

4. _____

5. _____

Scintillating Science

Studies show that expressing gratitude to others can significantly enhance our wellbeing. It can also have a powerful positive impact on the recipient and help strengthen the relationship. Research on the impact of a writing a gratitude letter (a letter of thanks in which gratitude is expressed to another person) has found that motivation to write the letter matters (Lyubomirsky, Dickerhoof, Boehm, & Sheldon, 2011).

Compared to non-motivated individuals, individuals who were highly motivated to write the gratitude letter (i.e. those who were clear on why they wanted to write it) reported improved overall wellbeing and fewer depressive symptoms at the end of the intervention. Motivated participants also showed improved wellbeing at the six-month follow up and reductions in depressive symptoms at the nine-month follow up (Seligman, Steen, Park, & Peterson, 2005).

This research highlights the importance of being clear on your motivation for undertaking the strategy and understanding whether the strategy is a good fit for you. If you are willing to trial it, you might find your motivation increases and you experience a positive impact on your wellbeing that you weren't expecting! You can read more on motivation in Week 2: Motivation.

Success Story

John, an educator, was a participant in one of our Positivity@Work workshops. As I introduced the topic of gratitude, highlighting the research findings and noting how easy it was to take things for granted, I noticed John's face begin to change. As a facilitator, you're attuned to the impact on the workshop participants of what you're saying or the videos you're playing, primarily through their facial expressions and their body language more broadly.

John didn't speak up that day. In fact, John became quieter and left the workshop without saying a word. When I returned for the second day of the workshop series in a month's time, I noticed John was sitting closer to the front and was smiling. When I asked for feedback on how the participants had gone in implementing the *Positivity Practices*, John was the first person to speak. He said, "Suzy, after watching that powerful video on gratitude, I realised that I had been taking my wife and children for granted. I drove straight home and told them individually and as a family just how much I loved them!"

He became quite emotional and shared with the group his commitment to spending more quality time with his family. He also mentioned that gratitude was one of his "lesser character strengths" and that he was actively going to work on making it a top strength from here on in (you can read more about character strengths in Week 3: Might).

Kindness

Research has provided strong evidence that being kind boosts our own levels of happiness and wellbeing and has a positive impact for the recipient. Acts of kindness are behaviours that benefit others or make others happy, typically at some cost to self.

There have been two primary approaches to studying the effects of kindness: pro-social spending, where participants are offered the opportunity to spend on others (often compared to groups who are instructed to spend on themselves), and acts of kindness, whereby participants are instructed to carry out acts of kindness for others (compared to self-kindness).

Research has found that both pro-social spending and acts of kindness for others boost happiness and wellbeing.

Positivity Practice #2: Counting Kindnesses

For this practice, I want you to become more aware of your own kind behaviour toward others. For the next week, try to perform at least five acts of kindness per day and record them in the evening in your journal, including any responses you received from others in performing the kind acts.

Examples include holding a door for someone, greeting strangers in the hallway or helping others at work. It doesn't matter if you perform kind acts towards those you know or those you don't know — research says you will still experience a boost to your wellbeing (Aknin, Dunn, & Norton, 2012).

Here are some kick-start ideas for acts of kindness:

• Give someone your seat on the bus or train.

• Hold a door open for someone.

• Give someone positive feedback or a compliment.

- Offer assistance to someone in need.

- Bake a cake for a friend or neighbour.

- Help someone with directions when they're lost.

- Pay a visit to a sick friend, relative or neighbour.

- Offer to look after a friend's child.

- Make your loved one breakfast in bed.

- Offer to do someone's shopping.

Scintillating Science

In a scientific study, students were randomly assigned to either a control group or an experimental group in which they were asked to perform five random acts of kindness a week for six weeks. The acts included such things as dropping coins into a stranger's parking meter, donating blood or visiting a sick relative. The students who engaged in acts of kindness were significantly happier than the controls at the end of the six weeks. The results of this intervention suggest that giving generates happiness. However, correlation does not equate to causality, so being in a positive mood may also make acts of kindness more likely (Lyubomirsky et al., 2005).

Forgiveness

Forgiveness is a sensitive and challenging topic for many people. There have been over 20 forgiveness interventions completed within the field of Positive Psychology. Generally, research has shown that granting forgiveness can be good for your wellbeing even if you do not let the other person know you have forgiven them. The effects are primarily to do with letting go of strong negative emotions, which are bad for our physical and psychological health.

For serious traumas and grievances, forgiveness can be complicated and can take time. Forgiveness may require the assistance of a professional to assist us through the process. For most of us though, there are daily opportunities to practice forgiveness in terms of letting things go and accepting that people are human and will sometimes say and do things, often unintentionally, that can disappoint us, hurt us or anger us.

People often hang onto grudges for a very long time rather than moving on. If you have been hurt by someone and believe you are still carrying strong negative emotions, it is important you process these emotions rather than let them simmer under the surface.

Note: If you've been the wrong-doer, research tells us that ruminating on your wrong-doing is bad for your physical health and psychological wellbeing. Recent research has shown that taking responsibility for your wrong-doing and seeking and receiving forgiveness helps reduce sadness and guilt (together with decreases in heart rate). Receiving forgiveness can come either from the victim in real life or imaginarily with self-forgiveness). Self-forgiveness is not about letting ourselves "off the hook" but is genuine, humble and responsible (da Silva, vanOyen Witvliet, & Riek, 2017).

Positivity Practice #3: Letting Go of Grudges

While forgiveness for serious transgressions often takes time and the help of a professional, letting go of smaller grudges past their use-by-date is worth considering. One model of forgiveness I have found useful is the REACH model (Worthington, 2008).

Dr Everett L. Worthington, Jr has developed a model that can help people learn how to forgive. Think of a person who has hurt you and apply the following steps to REACH forgiveness.

Recall the hurt. When we are hurt, we sometimes try to protect ourselves by denying our hurt. We think, often correctly, that if we do not think about it, it will not bother us. If unforgiveness keeps intruding into your happiness or gnawing ulcers in your gut, consider forgiving. Recall the hurt as objectively as possible. Do not rail against the person who hurt you, waste time wishing for an apology that will never be offered or dwell on your victimisation. Instead, admit that a wrong was done to you and set your sights on its repair.

Empathise. Empathy involves seeing things from another person's point of view, feeling that person's feelings and identifying with the pressures that made the person hurt you. To empathise with your offender's experience, write a brief letter to yourself as if you were the other person. How would he or she explain the harmful acts?

Altruistic gift of forgiveness. Empathy can prepare you for forgiving, but to give that gift of forgiveness, consider yourself. Have you ever harmed or offended a friend, a parent or a partner who later forgave you? Think about your guilt. Then consider the way you felt when you were forgiven. Most people say that they felt free, like chains were broken. Forgiveness can unshackle people from their guilt. By recalling your own guilt and the gratitude over being forgiven, you can develop the desire to give that gift of freedom to the person who hurt you.

Commit to forgive. When you forgive, you can eventually doubt that you have forgiven. When people remember a previous injury or offence, they often interpret it as evidence that they must not have forgiven. If you make your forgiveness tangible, you are less likely to doubt it later. Tell a friend, partner or counsellor that you have forgiven the person who hurt you. Write a certificate of forgiveness, stating that you have, as of today, forgiven.

Holding onto forgiveness. When you have doubts about whether you have forgiven, remind yourself of the forgiveness and tell yourself that a painful memory does not disqualify the hard work of forgiveness that you have done. Instead of trying to stop thoughts of unforgiveness, think positively about the forgiveness you have experienced. If you continue to doubt your forgiveness, work back through the REACH model.

Note: You might also like to undertake Dr Everett Worthington's online course on forgiveness if you think this topic is particularly relevant to you (www.evworthington-forgiveness.com/reach-resources). ✤

Scintillating Science

In one study, people were asked to think about someone who had hurt, mistreated or offended them while their blood pressure, heart rate, facial muscle tension and sweat gland activity were monitored (da Silva et al., 2017). When people recalled a grudge, their physical arousal soared, with their blood pressure, heart rate and sweat production increasing. Ruminating about their grudges was stressful and subjects found the rumination unpleasant. It made them feel angry, sad, anxious and less in control.

In the same study, participants were asked to empathise with their offenders or imagine forgiving them. When they practised forgiveness, their physical arousal dropped. They showed no more of a stress reaction than everyday life produces.

Success Story

After learning about the power of forgiveness and the scientific support for its practice, Anna, a student in one of my classes, chose forgiveness as a *Positivity Practice* she wanted to put to the test. Anna's father, who had recently passed on, had a major falling out with his brother when Anna was a child. This falling out led to Anna's parents moving country and cutting all ties with the family. This meant Anna never had a chance to meet her uncle, his wife and their family in her adolescence and young adulthood. When Anna's father died, Anna decided she would attempt to locate her uncle (who would now be in his eighties) if he was still alive. Whilst Anna never really knew the reasons for the family feud, she knew her father had held onto a lot of anger for many years and had taken that anger to his deathbed.

To her surprise, her uncle responded immediately when she reached out, showing enormous remorse for not contacting her father years earlier and especially before he died. Anna herself didn't feel anger towards her uncle. She felt that forgiveness was needed to mend long-held family discord. Anna was able to give her uncle the opportunity to take responsibility for his actions and she expressed forgiveness to him, something which hadn't occurred while her father was alive. This act of forgiveness created a powerful positive ripple effect across both families and resurrected the family structure.

Week 1 Challenge Checklist

By the end of Week 1 you should have:

☐ **Counted your blessings.** Use a gratitude journal or app to cultivate gratitude every night this week. Do not beat yourself up if you do not complete it every night as you should still experience some benefits. Research has shown that practising gratitude only once a week can significantly boost your mood in as little as a month!

☐ **Counted your daily kindnesses.** Use your journal to record at least five acts of kindness every day this week.

☐ **Let go of a grudge.** Identify someone that you hold a grudge towards and use the REACH forgiveness model to let go of the grudge. Do not forget to take some time to reassess at the end of the week how you feel about that person and how you feel about yourself.

Week 2: Motivation

"To infinity and beyond."

BUZZ LIGHTYEAR

Welcome to Week 2: Motivation, where we'll explore the process of change and help you increase your intrinsic motivation, the key to sustained change.

This week we'll look at:

- The science of change.

- The stages of change to help you identify where you're at right now (it may not be action!).

- Your reasons for change to help you understand the importance of intrinsic motivation.

- Leveraging the power of values and an inspirational vision in becoming your best self.

So, are you ready for change? Are you ready to be your best self? How would you rate your current level of motivation to do this on a scale from 1 to 10 (where 1 is no motivation and 10 is highly motivated)?

What about your commitment? Can you clearly articulate why you are embarking on this program?

These are important questions when it comes to your motivation, not only to start the program but to stay the course until you create the positive changes you desire and, more importantly, sustain those changes for the long term.

But don't worry too much if you can't answer all these questions right now as we will be covering them in detail this week.

Scientifically speaking, we know that:

- Change is not easy, otherwise everyone would make the changes they desire.

- There are different stages of change that we progress through towards successful and sustained change.

- Relapse (i.e. returning to your old patterns of behaviour) is normal.

- There are proven strategies you can use to move toward success, even after relapse.

Motivation is a big topic and it has been written about in every professional domain from sports to education. Motivation underpins everything we do, including why we get out of bed in the morning or not (particularly when it comes to those doona days!). We also know that when we are not feeling good, lack of motivation is common. The worst-case scenario can be debilitating as many people with clinical depression will attest to. Not only is there a loss of motivation, but you can also experience a loss of pleasure in activities that were once pleasurable.

Even if you are not depressed, most people struggle with maintaining motivation on a daily basis. Even the most motivated people will tell you that their motivation waxes and wanes. I want you to know that this is completely normal.

What can you do to give yourself a good dose of motivation to kick-start the program, but more importantly, to see it through to the end? There are two key factors to consider when we are contemplating change, whether this is in regard to stopping a bad habit or starting a positive one. These are readiness for change and reasons for change.

Are You Really Ready?

Just because you set an intention for change (e.g. to prioritise positivity), this does not mean that you are really ready for change. There is a significant amount of science, mostly from drug and alcohol research, to support the notion that there are different stages of change that people go through and that it is possible to assess our readiness for change.

Early research on readiness for change also focused on diet and exercise. In one large study of gyms, people's readiness for change was assessed when they first signed up for their membership (Prochaska & DiClemente, 1983). What this research uncovered was that the majority of people were not ready for action; they were only contemplating change.

We also know that if we treat people as if they're ready for action when they're only at contemplation, we can potentially demotivate them or lose their engagement in the change process.

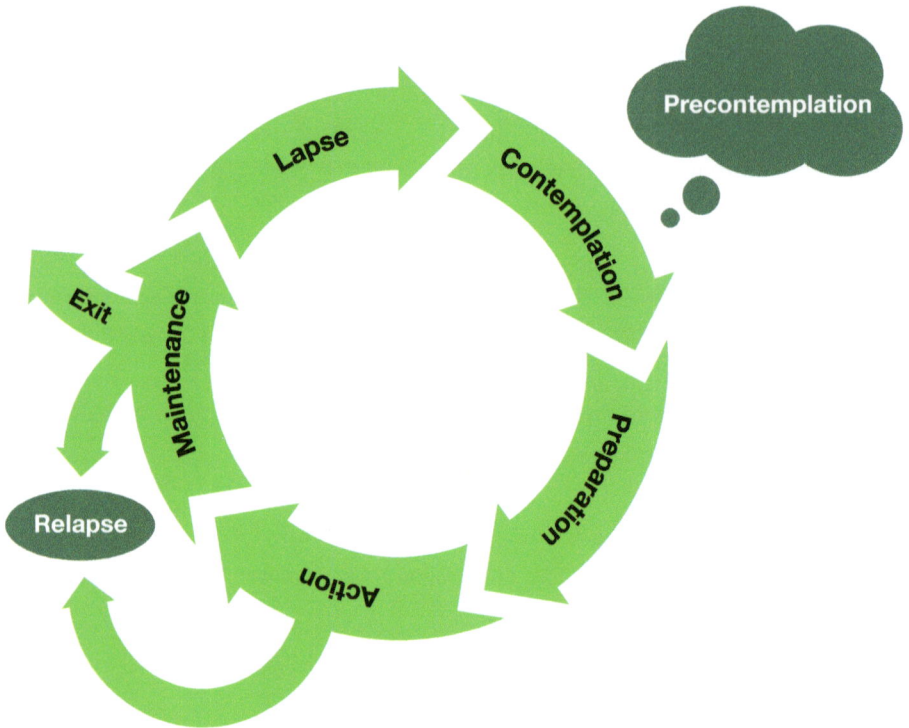

Stages of Change Model

The graphic depicts the six primary stages of change: precontemplation, contemplation, preparation, action, maintenance and relapse (Prochaska & DiClemente, 1983). Now is the time to determine which stage of change you are at before beginning this program. While you may have specific goals in mind for this program, try to reflect more on your general stage of change in terms of completing the program, improving your mood and applying the strategies to create a flourishing life.

Stage of change	Description
Precontemplation	I have not considered making changes to improve my life and I do not intend to in the near future.
Contemplation	I have thought about making positive changes in my life to improve my wellbeing but have not done anything concrete about it.
Preparation	I am intending to (or have commenced in the past week) to make some changes in my life that will have a positive impact on my wellbeing.
Action	I have been actively making changes in my life for at least the last month and have seen and felt the impact on my wellbeing.
Maintenance	I have been actively making successful changes in my life that have positively impacted my wellbeing for the last six months.
Relapse	I had started to make real changes and feel better but have slipped back to my old ways and now notice that I am not feeling as good as I was.

My current stage of change is: _____

Let's analyse your results now:

Precontemplators are often blissfully ignorant of the need for change. It's often not until they reach rock bottom that they reach out for help or a partner gives them an ultimatum in regard to making change. It's unlikely you're a precontemplator given you've bought this book, which is an indication in itself of readiness for change. You may however be quite cynical about its contents or your expectations of what it can deliver. Even though you may not feel ready to change right now, reading this book and finding out more information may help you move to the next stage of contemplation.

Contemplators have come to the realisation they need to change but they don't necessarily want to change yet. They're weighing up the pros and cons of change. The good news is that reading this book will hopefully help you realise that the pros outweigh any cons and that life's too short to languish!

If you are in **preparation**, you're getting ready for change. You've bought the book, you've been reading about how others have made successful change and you are thinking about how much better life will be with the changes you intend to make. In this stage, it's important you develop a plan and find support. *The Positivity Prescription* will assist you in creating a plan that will work for you. In addition, engaging a coach can also be a great step in this phase, particularly in helping you follow through with it.

Are you ready for **action**? If so, you're on your way and are most likely already making changes that are positively affecting your wellbeing, including completing this program. In the action stage though, it's important to realise that relapse is possible and in fact likely. You will require support to stay on track. Now is the time to be proactive and consider engaging a coach (even if it's just for the next six months) until the *Positivity Practices* become habitual and you have sustained the change you desired.

Or you might be in the **maintenance phase**. You have made changes for over six months and want to maintain those changes for the rest of your life. Even when the next curve ball comes, you feel confident that you can handle it and that you can maintain a state of flourishing through life's ups and downs. Purchasing the book may in fact be an action that you've taken to help reinforce all the positive changes you've already made and support sustainability.

Please don't worry if you find yourself at **contemplation, preparation** or even **relapse**. In fact, I'm assuming that most people will be in one of those stages when buying the book. The good news is that there are powerful steps you can take to move to action and this is what *The Positivity Prescription* is designed to do, particularly in this Module. We will be focusing on maintenance and discussing relapse towards the end of the program.

The Importance of Intrinsic Motivation

In this Module, my aim is to introduce you to the primary principles of motivation and specifically to a scientific concept known as *intrinsic motivation*, the secret to your success.

In a nutshell, intrinsic motivation means you're doing this program for yourself, first and foremost. No one is insisting or forcing you to make changes. The primary reason you have decided to commit to this program and your goals is because it's important to you to feel good, function well and live your best life. I will also introduce you to scientifically proven strategies to increase intrinsic motivation, even if you are extrinsically motivated to begin with.

In years of consulting with clients, I have found that people who are extrinsically motivated (i.e. when people pursue goals that are not truly their own) do so for two reasons. One is that there are goals we are told we must pursue. This happens a lot in the workplace where we are required to work towards key performance indicators given to us when we do not have the option to say no to the boss. We often feel forced into doing these tasks, like we have no choice. I have also seen this happen often when it comes to our health, for example, when the doctor advises us to lose weight or start exercising.

It can also happen when it comes to our mood. We might receive feedback from our partner, family or friends that we've not been our usual self or our best self in quite a while. They've most likely been experiencing the effects of your bad mood, perhaps through your lack of desire for fun, playfulness, joy and overall positive engagement in life. We know from research that emotions are contagious and your mood has most likely affected their mood and motivation!

The other reason we are extrinsically motivated is because we think it is what is expected of us. Sometimes we pursue goals because someone thinks we should, such as our partner or our parents, but if we did not feel so much guilt and were being true to ourselves, we probably would not pursue this goal.

This is really important when it comes to completing this program, because this might be your primary reason. We believe we *should* be in a better mood. We *should* be happy. But as you'll soon find out, your primary reason has to be because you wholeheartedly want to. That is, you're the one choosing to complete the program and you're really clear on why you're doing it for you. You want to do it, but don't feel like you should be doing it. This might mean that you're doing it because you want to have positive relationships and a positive energising effect on others.

My aim for you in this program is to give you every tool that will support your success. This means that you will need to know the why behind the desires, dreams or changes you want to make to improve your wellbeing. In the morning, during the day and in the evening over the course of the next six weeks, when your motivation wanes (and it will), you will have to keep reminding yourself of why you are committed to this program. It cannot be because someone else wants you to do it and you will let them down if you fail.

Research tells us that for you to succeed at your goals, your motivation needs to be intrinsic, not extrinsic, which means you cannot be doing this for anyone else but you.

Are You Intrinsically Motivated?

Use the questions below to reflect on your motivation to complete *The Positivity Prescription* in relation to the intrinsic-extrinsic continuum. Questions 1 and 2 reflect extrinsic motivation and questions 3 and 4 reflect intrinsic motivation. You may find that your motivation falls into more than one category. At this point, it is important to be honest because even if you discover you are extrinsically motivated, spending time focusing on your values and vision will help you move towards a greater level of intrinsic motivation.

1. I am completing *The Positivity Prescription* because somebody else wants me to or thinks I ought to, or because I will get something from somebody if I do. That is, I probably would not do the program if I did not get a reward, praise or approval for it.

Rating: 1   2   3   4   5   6   7   8   9   1 0

2. I am completing *The Positivity Prescription* because I would feel guilty or anxious if I did not. Rather than striving because someone else thinks I ought to, I feel that I should strive to complete the program.

Rating: 1   2   3   4   5   6   7   8   9   1 0

3. I am completing *The Positivity Prescription* because I believe it is an important goal to have. Although completing the program may once have been suggested to me by others, I now see the value in completing it and I am embracing the program wholeheartedly.

Rating: 1   2   3   4   5   6   7   8   9   1 0

4. I am completing *The Positivity Prescription* because of the fun and enjoyment I know I will experience. While there may be many good reasons to complete the program, the primary reason I am doing it is simply because of my interest in the experience itself.

Rating: 1   2   3   4   5   6   7   8   9   1 0

Reference: Adapted from Emmons (1986).

Take some time to jot down in your journal your reasons for commencing and completing *The Positivity Prescription*. If you find your motivation is more extrinsic than intrinsic, read on as you'll hopefully find you'll be moving more towards being intrinsically motivated as we progress through the program.

Scintillating Science

Self-determination theory explores a person's reasons for pursuing their goals and distinguishes between autonomous and controlled motivation (Deci & Ryan, 2008). Autonomous motivation involves a sense of choice (i.e. intrinsic motivation). Controlled motivation involves feeling pressured or coerced by others or our own internal forces, such as guilt or anxiety (i.e. extrinsic motivation).

Self-determination theory also focuses on the authenticity of our goals. Research suggests that the more our short-term goals reflect our underlying values and interests and connect to our possible futures, the more likely we will attain our goals and experience success (Sheldon, Kasser, Smith, & Share, 2002; Sheldon & Elliot, 1999).

Becoming More Intrinsically Motivated

Research has uncovered four strategies that can help us increase our intrinsic motivation and help us feel more autonomous in the pursuit of our goals (Sheldon et al., 2002).

Own your goal. In this strategy, think back to times when you may have had difficulties with a goal. Try to identify the deeper or core values that the goal represents (e.g. health or relationships). You'll be reading more about core values this week and you'll be spending more time identifying your values, but for now, just try and identify the "why" of your goal.

Make it fun. In this strategy, the aim is to make the goal or *Positivity Practices* as much fun as possible. For example, the goal of improving your mood might be enhanced by undertaking this program with a friend or by identifying settings in which undertaking the *Positivity Practices* might be more enjoyable (e.g. in a café) or challenging (doing more than what you've been asked to do, such as enacting 10 random acts of kindness in one day rather than 5).

Remember the big picture. In this strategy, spend some time reflecting on the longer-term goals that your current goal serves. For example, recalling the broader purpose of improving your mood is to be able to function at your best and achieve your other life goals, like getting into the course you've always wanted or creating the life of your dreams.

Keep a balance. This strategy is about spreading your efforts among all your goals, or in this case, it might mean spreading your efforts over the numerous *Positivity Practices* you're being introduced to. The main thing to note here is that it's really important to spend time doing things you enjoy in order to avoid burnout. For example, your goal of improving your mood will definitely be enhanced by you simultaneously pursuing your physical health and fitness goals, such as exercising more often or sticking to a healthy eating plan.

The overall aim here is to make your goals more meaningful. Research has found that there are clear differences in how personal and impersonal goals feel as they are pursued (Sheldon et al., 2002). If you've discovered you're mainly undertaking this program for extrinsic reasons, then you may have already been experiencing uncomfortable feelings. Rather than trying to avoid or escape these feelings, you might like to consider using one or more of the four strategies to help increase your intrinsic motivation. Intrinsic motivation feels right and is energising.

For now, reflect on the importance of both readiness for change and reasons for change. Jot down your results in undertaking the questionnaires in your journal and continue to reflect on your reasons for change.

What About Willpower?

Even if you think you are intrinsically motivated, are you still feeling anxious about whether you will succeed in this program? Perhaps you think you haven't got what it takes to see it through. You may have a stack of negative thoughts about your capacity to achieve your goals (we'll tackle those in Week 6: Mindset).

If you have any of these concerns, you are probably thinking you don't have much willpower. The good news is that recent research highlights the vital role of intrinsic motivation in bolstering willpower and mitigating mental fatigue during goal pursuit. As you've discovered, intrinsic motivation is driven by personal enjoyment, curiosity, or meaning and provides a sustainable source of energy and focus. Studies show that when individuals engage in tasks they find intrinsically motivating, they perceive them as less effortful and experience lower levels of fatigue, even after extended periods of exertion (Muraven, & Slessareva, 2003).

Being clear on your reasons for implementing the Positivity Practices and reminding yourself regularly of your "why" will ensure you remain intrinsically motivated and enhance your overall chances of success.

Hope: The Waypower

In addition to intrinsic motivation and willpower, you'll need hope. People hold very different beliefs and emotions about hope, particularly false hope, but it's important to know that hope is a well-validated scientific theory. Research has shown there are individual differences when it comes to hope, with some people having very high levels of hope and others having quite low levels of hope, which is often the case in clinical depression.

A "high hoper" is a person who sets a number of personally meaningful goals, not just one. They have significant amounts of willpower, motivation and self-control, but more importantly, they have "waypower". This means they identify and create multiple options, plans and pathways to achieve their goals and dreams. "High hopers" don't rely on just one plan, they have plans B, C, D and E nailed down, often before they even commence their goal pursuits.

Research has shown that children, adolescents and adults with higher levels of hope do better in school and athletics, have better health, have better problem-solving skills and are better adjusted psychologically (Snyder, 2002; Snyder, Michael, & Cheavens, 1999). Overall, hope is something to cultivate and when it comes to motivation, you will definitely need to be a "high hoper" to complete the program.

Hope has three core components:

Goals. Not just any goals, but personally meaningful, authentic and values-congruent goals. We've just covered the concept of intrinsic motivation, and in this week's homework, you'll be spending more time on clarifying your values.

Agency. The willpower, the mindset and thinking that can either support your success or undermine it. We'll be spending a lot of time on mindset in Week 6: Mindset. For now, start to become more mindful of your automatic negative thoughts (ANTS) and whether they are helping you or hindering you! Keep a note of them in your journal.

Pathways. The waypower, the options and strategies that you can use to achieve your end goal. By the end of this program, you'll have a stack of strategies to help you increase your wellbeing and create a flourishing life.
Answer the questions below with a simple yes or no to help you reflect on whether you're a high hoper:

1. If I find myself in a pickle, I can think of many ways to get out of it.

2. At the present time, I am energetically pursuing my goals.

3. There are many ways around any problem that I am facing.

4. Currently, I see myself as being pretty successful.

5. I can think of many ways to reach my current goals.

6. At this time, I am meeting the goals I have set for myself.

The questions that uncover agency are questions 2, 4 and 6. The questions that uncover pathways are questions 1, 3 and 5. Don't be too concerned if in answering these questions, you've discovered you don't have high levels of willpower (agency) or waypower. The whole aim of the *The Positivity Prescription* is to help you become a high hoper!

Reference: Snyder, C. R., Sympson, S. C., Ybasco, F. C., Borders, T. F., Babyak, M. A., & Higgins, R. L. (1996). Development and validation of the State Hope Scale. *Journal of Personality and Social Psychology*, 2, 321-335.

Values

As you've been learning, intrinsic motivation is the secret sauce when it comes to success. In my work with clients, the most powerful tool I have used to enhance intrinsic motivation and create major shifts in behaviour is through the identification of core values. Not only does clarifying core values assist with motivation for the attainment of specific goals but this powerful exercise changes lives!

For many clients, completing a core values exercise can lead to major "aha" moments and the realisation that they have not been living an authentic life based on their values. For many people, this lack of an authentic life may have led to physical illness and/or psychological distress.

While the rapidly expanding field of psychoneuroimmunology (how the mind and emotions affect our physical body) supports this idea, I have seen time and time again in my work that clients suffer physically and mentally when living a values-incongruent life. I have also seen the powerful impact that clarifying values can have for people, and more importantly, the positive and beneficial effects that living a values-congruent life can have, even with small steps in that direction.

Values are a foundational piece in *The Positivity Prescription* and in living a flourishing life. Values can be differentiated from needs in that they are not essential to our physical or mental health. However, we place importance on them and make meaning out of them. They also form the basis for our choices of action. Values are important when it comes to both our short- and long-term goals because they give us some insight as to how we want to live.

There hasn't been a large amount of research conducted on values, however the research we do have tells us that they've often been inherited via our family upbringing or via our important relationships. We might adopt the values of someone whom we respect. Whilst our early values are often learned or taught to us by our parents or family, it's often during adolescence or early adulthood that we adopt new values or let go of family values (although this may be temporary and we may re-adopt these at a later stage of life). Going through difficult times can also help us gain clarity on what really matters, or what doesn't, as the case may be.

Positivity Practice #4: Crystallising and Prioritising Values

This *Positivity Practice* involves identifying your top five core life values. Following on we've provided a list of values. It is not exhaustive so feel free to add your own values to the list. We have our own set of values cards at The Positivity Institute (www.thepositivityinstitute.com.au) that you can purchase to assist you in this exercise. The cards can be helpful in as much as you can sort them into "very important", "not so important" and "not quite sure" piles.

Jenny, a workshop participant, told me that she put her values cards on her lounge-room floor each night for a week and when she came home in the evening, she moved the cards around with her foot (and a glass of wine in hand) until she finally felt happy with her top five life values. A great way to complete the exercise!

Using the list below, I would suggest you first tick all the values that you believe are important to you. Then go back over the list a second, third or fourth time and work on prioritising them. I recommend that you do this until you can name your top five values, hopefully by the end of the week.

In my experience, most people have never given much thought to their values and it may take up to a month to get clarity. In fact, one client mentioned that she needed a year to get clarity on her values!

Once you have identified your values, spend some time in meditation reflecting on them. They should feel right to you. Many people experience a strong physical feeling of rightness once they identify their top five.

Values Crystallisation and Prioritisation

Acceptance	Flexibility	Persistence
Adventure	Forgiveness	Pleasure
Affection	Freedom	Positivity
Altruism	Friendship	Power
Ambition	Fun	Purpose
Assertiveness	Generosity	Recognition
Authenticity	Gentleness	Relationships
Autonomy	Gratitude	Respect
Balance	Growth	Romance
Beauty	Happiness	Safety
Belonging	Harmony	Self-awareness
Choice	Health	Self-compassion
Collaboration	Honesty	Self-determination
Commitment	Humility	Self-respect
Communication	Humor	Sensitivity
Community	Influence	Serenity
Compassion	Integrity	Service
Competence	Intimacy	Simplicity
Confidence	Intuition	Solitude
Consistency	Kindness	Spirituality
Contentment	Leadership	Success
Contribution	Learning	Support
Courage	Legacy	Teamwork
Creativity	Love	Tolerance
Curiosity	Loyalty	Tradition
Dependability	Mindfulness	Trust
Discipline	Nature	Variety
Diversity	Nurturing	Vitality
Education	Open-mindedness	Wealth
Empowerment	Optimism	Wellbeing
Enthusiasm	Order	Wisdom
Equality	Passion	
Excellence	Patience	
Family	Peace	

Your top five core life values:

1. _____

2. _____

3. _____

4. _____

5. _____

Success Story

One of my very first coaching clients was a partner in an accounting firm. Jim had contacted me for executive coaching to improve his work-life balance. Sue, his wife, had significant concerns and frustrations about his long working hours. Jim generally left early in the morning before the children were awake and arrived home later at night after they were asleep, leaving little time for Jim and Sue to relax and reflect on the day. Sue was concerned for her relationship and her family's wellbeing.

After clarifying Jim's goal to improve his work-life balance, the first activity I prescribed was to clarify his core life values. Jim held religious beliefs and for him the exercise was relatively easy. He explained to me he knew what mattered most, but he had lost sight of this in his pursuit for career success. He also realised that although his career progression was really about supporting his family, his commitment to success was unwittingly impacting on the very value he was trying to fulfil, his family. Jim realised that his number one core value of family needed to stay front and centre of his mind and his life.

Jim was able to make changes to his working schedule to ensure he was home earlier in the evening with his family but also make the career progress he desired. Jim shared with me that his core life values became his guiding lights. With his top five values clear, every decision he made became easier as he used his values to determine what was right for him and his family.

Vision

To create change, we require an inspirational vision. Developing a inspirational vision of the future is really about dreaming of what you'd like your life to look and feel like in the long term, ideally 5 to 10 years. It's also about developing a vision of who you want to be, or need to be, to help create that vision.

Sometimes, our vision is larger than life, for example, solving world hunger or undertaking intergalactic space travel. That's okay too. It's about tapping into your dreams and desires and helping you see how your vision is aligned to your values.

In developing your vision, I'm going to ask you to give yourself permission to dream. With clarity on your values, it is important you start developing an inspirational, yet fuzzy vision of your future where you are your best possible self.

Inspirational, because if it is not, why bother? Fuzzy, because our vision cannot be too rigid or immovable as life changes and we often have to change course. An inspirational vision that has values woven into it provides flexibility, so that even if the vision does not turn out exactly as we had imagined, if we are living our values, then we will still experience high levels of wellbeing.

There are a number of reasons why creating a vision is important, not only in terms of enhancing your chances of creating the future you desire, but also in terms of reducing your anxieties and worries about what might happen in the future. It's also been shown to enhance your psychological wellbeing. In the book, *The Present*, by Spencer Johnson, the author suggests that creating a vision of the future gives our brain something to work with and as such allows us to limit the "what ifs", creating more contentment in the process.

The other benefit of creating a vision of the future is it allows us to be more in the present, knowing that we have a plan for the future. There have been a large number of scientific papers that have provided evidence for the benefits of being present and living in the now, particularly for mental health. This is something the Buddhists have known for centuries. (We will be learning more about Mindfulness in Week 5).

Developing a fuzzy vision also primes our brain to notice opportunities to create that vision. Opportunities we may otherwise not have identified become clear to us and we find and develop plans and pathways that instil hope to create our fuzzy vision.

How often have you overheard a conversation or something caught your eye in a magazine that you wanted to learn about or do that you would have otherwise ignored if you had not already started to give thought to these ideas?

In the scientific literature, this phenomenon is referred to as the attentional bias. Attentional bias is the tendency of our perception to be affected by our recurring thoughts and this is a very real scientific fact.

Positivity Practice #5: Letter from the Future

Developing a vision can be done through an automatic writing process, such as a letter from a future you, or through a creative process, such as developing a vision board or a treasure map using pictures and symbols. This *Positivity Practice* involves writing a letter from your future self, describing your flourishing future life in 5 to 10 years' time.

Remember, it is important to keep it fuzzy and to write about how you are living your values. If you are not a natural writer, you can create a vision board or a treasure map that is a visual and artistic expression of your fuzzy vision. The important thing is that you give yourself permission to dream.

Choose a date in the future and imagine that you have travelled in time and are sitting down writing a letter to yourself. Tell yourself how great your life is now and how you have managed to get rid of so many of those things that were irritating you or draining you. Write about how you are truly flourishing and experiencing high levels of psychological wellbeing. When you write this letter, rather than focusing on the negative (the things you do not want in your life), write about what you would really love to happen. Focus on the solution, not the problem or the absence of a problem.

You might also like to use a Life Balance Wheel like the one below to ensure your letter covers all the important areas of your life such as career, social activities, relationships, finances and spirituality.

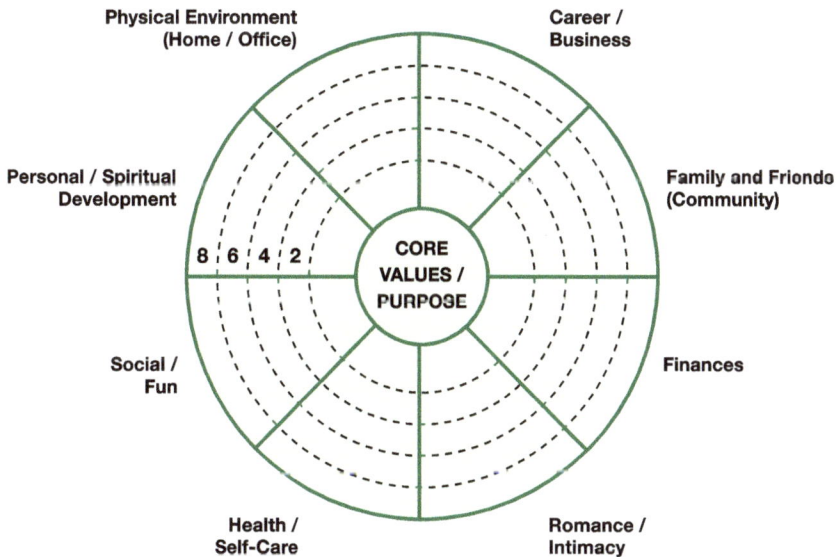

Physical Environment (Home / Office) · Career / Business · Personal / Spiritual Development · Family and Friends (Community) · CORE VALUES / PURPOSE · 8 6 4 2 · Social / Fun · Finances · Health / Self-Care · Romance / Intimacy

The Letter from the Future is a simple and powerful tool for change. Many of my clients have been amazed at the results they have achieved using this technique, sometimes in much less than 5 to 10 years' time. One client found one of his longer-term goals coming true six months after he wrote the letter when he found the home of his dreams at a price he could afford.

Note: This practice was adapted from an activity outlined in Grant, A. M., & Greene, J. (2001). Coach Yourself: Make real change in your life. London, England: Momentum Press. ✼

Success Story

This story is one of my own. I wrote my first Letter from the Future 20 years ago, in my early thirties. I had clarified my top five core values and wrote about how I wanted my life to look and who I wanted to become over the next 10 years. I read and re-read that letter regularly over the 10 years.

When I reached the future date, I recognised that much of what I had described, had come to fruition. However, there were still things I'd written about that hadn't occurred. I decided to keep the letter and change the date for another five years into the future. At the end of the next five years, more things had happened! It wasn't magic, it was just that I had consciously (and unconsciously) worked on the goals I had identified over that time frame.

I then wrote another Letter from the Future when I turned 50. This letter was more mature, sophisticated but also braver and bigger. As I get older, I realise that time flies and life truly is too short to languish. I have a weekly Sunday morning ritual where I review my values and my vision (my Letter from the Future) and then set goals for the week ahead that help me move towards that vision. So far, so good!

Week 2 Challenge Checklist

By the end of Week 2 you should have:

☐ Determined your stage of change and readiness for change.

☐ Identified your reasons for change.

☐ Crystallised and prioritised your top five core life values.

☐ Written your Letter from the Future to create an inspirational fuzzy vision.

Week 3: Might

"Look well into thyself; there is a source of strength which will always spring up if thou wilt always look there."

MARCUS AURELIUS

Welcome to Week 3: Might, where we'll be focusing on our strengths to experience more energy and become our best possible self.

_____

This week, we will look at:

- What strengths are.

- Why developing our character strengths is so important.

- Why developing lesser strengths is also encouraged.

- How to spot strengths to build positive relationships.

Why Might Matters

While we have all heard the adage "play to your strengths", in the field of Positive Psychology, the scientific study of strengths has become a core component of understanding and creating a flourishing life.

Character strengths are positive individual traits reflected in thoughts, feelings and behaviours. This is similar to personality traits but different in that strengths are morally valued cross-culturally. Character strengths include broad concepts such as forgiveness, love, kindness, leadership and gratitude. Research tells us that knowing and using our strengths impacts positively on a range of outcomes including goal attainment, wellbeing and energy.

Let's look at three approaches to leveraging strengths:

- **Strengths knowledge.** Assessing and understanding your character strengths.

- **Strengths use.** Using scientific strategies to put your strengths to work and increase your performance, wellbeing and energy.

- **Strengths spotting.** Using strengths as a lens through which to see other people and develop positive relationships.

Strengths Knowledge

Many people find it a challenge to identify their strengths although they can very easily tell you about their weaknesses and areas for development. This is why a strengths assessment can be helpful in better understanding your strengths. There are many strengths assessments available, but many are not scientifically supported. There are also different approaches to assessing strengths, generally categorised into character strengths and performance strengths. In this program, we will focus on character strengths.

Character Strengths

The VIA (Values in Action) classification of strengths was developed in 2004 and was originally created by Professors Chris Peterson and Martin Seligman, the founding fathers of Positive Psychology. The VIA classification of strengths classifies psychological strengths rather than weaknesses, what most Psychologists have focused on in the past.

Character strengths are defined as "the psychological ingredients, processes or mechanisms that define the virtues" (Peterson & Seligman, 2004). Virtues are core characteristics valued by moral philosophers and religious thinkers, such as wisdom and justice. Researchers suggest virtues exist in degrees and individual differences exist. It has been speculated that virtues are grounded in biology through an evolutionary process that selected for these predispositions towards moral excellence as a means of survival (Park et al., 2004).

The VIA Classification

The VIA classification system describes individual differences in character strengths on a continuum, as opposed to distinct categories. The classification is, therefore, sensitive to the contexts in which character strengths are displayed and deployed. There are six categories or "virtue clusters" delineated in the VIA classification system: wisdom, courage, humanity, justice, temperance and transcendence. These represent universal and cross-cultural virtues.

Virtues

Wisdom	creativity, curiosity, open-mindedness, love of learning and perspective
Courage	bravery, persistence, integrity and vitality
Humanity	love, kindness and social intelligence
Justice	citizenship, fairness and leadership
Temperance	forgiveness, humility, prudence and self-regulation
Transcendence	appreciation of beauty and excellence, gratitude, hope, humour and spirituality

The 24 VIA character strengths contribute to the six virtues described above. The criteria for defining a character strength are that it must be seen across different situations over time and must be valued in its own right, not only for its positive consequences. The VIA strengths survey rank orders your 24 strengths and highlights your top five signature strengths, your middle strengths and your lesser strengths (not necessarily weaknesses!).

This assessment is available on the following website (www.viacharacter.org) and you can get a free report or a more extensive paid report.

Professor Seligman (2002) suggests that you review your top five signature strengths and, for each, ask yourself if any of the following criteria apply:

- A sense of ownership and authenticity ("This is the real me").

- A feeling of excitement, energy and joy when displaying the strength, particularly at first ("This is me at my best").

- A feeling of inevitability in using the strength ("Try to stop me").

We also usually find that people unknowingly create and pursue goals and personal projects that revolve around their strengths. Most people resonate with the increased energy, authenticity and joy in using their strengths. Personally, "zest, energy and vitality" is my top strength and I realised that as I have moved towards doing work I loved over the years, the more energy I experienced.

Signature strengths are what define us and these are easily spotted in us by others, particularly those we know well. There has been a significant amount of research on the value of identifying and using our signature strengths (Buckingham & Clifton, 2001; Peterson & Seligman, 2004).

The 24 VIA Character Strengths

Character strength	Strength-related traits
Appreciation of beauty and excellence	Awe, wonder and elevation: noticing and appreciating beauty, excellence and/or skilled performance in various domains of life, from nature, art, mathematics and science to everyday experience.
Bravery	Valour and courage: not shrinking from threat, challenge, difficulty or pain; speaking up for what is right even if there is opposition; acting on convictions even if unpopular; includes physical bravery but is not limited to it.
Creativity	Originality and ingenuity: thinking of novel and productive ways to conceptualise and do things; includes artistic achievement but is not limited to it.
Curiosity	Interest in the world, novelty-seeking and openness to experience: taking an interest in ongoing experience for its own sake; finding subjects and topics fascinating; exploring and discovering.
Fairness	Equity and justice: treating all people the same according to notions of fairness and justice; not letting personal feelings bias decisions about others; giving everyone a fair chance.
Forgiveness	Mercy; forgiving those who have done wrong; accepting the shortcomings of others; giving people a second chance; not being vengeful.

Character strength	Strength-related traits
Gratitude	Being aware of and thankful for the good things that happen; taking time to express thanks.
Honesty	Authenticity and integrity: speaking the truth, but more broadly, presenting yourself in a genuine way and acting in a sincere way; being without pretence; taking responsibility for your feelings and actions.
Hope	Optimism, future mindedness and future orientation: expecting the best in the future and working to achieve it; believing that a good future is something that can be brought about.
Humility	Letting your accomplishments speak for themselves and not regarding yourself as more special than you are.
Humour	Playfulness: liking to laugh and tease; bringing smiles to other people; seeing the light side; making jokes.
Kindness	Generosity: kindness is akin to care, compassion, altruistic love and niceness. It is doing favours and good deeds for others, helping them and taking care of them.
Leadership	Encouraging a group of which you are a member to get things done and at the same time, maintain good relations within the group; organising group activities and overseeing that they happen.

Character strength	Strength-related traits
Love	Capacity to love and be loved: valuing close relationships with others, in particular those in which sharing and caring are reciprocated; being close to people.
Love of learning	Mastering new skills, topics and bodies of knowledge, whether on your own or formally; related to the strength of curiosity but goes beyond it to describe the tendency to add systematically to what you know.
Open-mindedness	Judgement and critical thinking: thinking things through and examining them from all sides; not jumping to conclusions; being able to change your mind in light of evidence; weighing all evidence fairly.
Persistence	Perseverance, industriousness and diligence: finishing what you start; persisting in a course of action in spite of the obstacles; taking pleasure in completing tasks.
Perspective	Wisdom: being able to provide wise counsel to others; having ways of looking at the world that make sense to yourself and other people.
Prudence	Caution and discretion: being careful about your choices; not taking undue risks; not saying or doing things that might later be regretted.
Self-Regulation	Self-control: regulating what you feel and do; being disciplined; controlling your appetites and emotions.

Character strength	Strength-related traits
Social intelligence	Friendship, emotional intelligence and personal intelligence: being aware of the motives and feelings of other people and yourself; knowing what to do to fit in different social situations; knowing what makes other people tick.
Spirituality	Faith and sense of purpose: having coherent beliefs about the higher purpose and meaning of the universe; knowing where you fit within the larger scheme; having beliefs about the meaning of life that shape your conduct and provide comfort.
Teamwork	Citizenship, loyalty and social responsibility: working well as a member of a group or team; being loyal to the group; doing your share.
Zest	Vigour, excitement and energy; not doing things half-heartedly; living life as an adventure; feeling alive and activated.

The Golden Five

An early study on character strengths found that hope, zest, gratitude, love and curiosity were most strongly correlated with life satisfaction (Park, Peterson, & Seligman, 2004). These became known as the "golden five".

With this knowledge in mind, many people scanned their results to see where these strengths sat on their ranked VIA assessment results. Were they "signature strengths" or "lesser strengths"? In working with clients over the years, I have noticed that those experiencing lower levels of wellbeing do tend to have these strengths located in the bottom half of their VIA results. It made sense to me too, as those suffering with depression tend to experience the opposite of hope (hopelessness), zest (lethargy), gratitude (difficulty identifying what's working well), love (feeling unloved) and curiosity (engaging in black and white thinking).

I always tell my clients the good news is that these character strengths can be developed. For example:

Hope. In my own research on evidence-based coaching, I have been able to show that coaching (the setting and striving towards personally meaningful goals through a supportive coaching relationship) was in fact a hope-enhancement intervention (Grant, Green, & Rynsaardt, 2010). We'll be doing some of that towards the end of the program.

Zest. Whilst research on the topic of zest, energy and vitality is limited, research on the use of strengths has shown that strengths use is highly correlated with increased levels of vitality (Govindji & Linley, 2007). As we'll learn though, knowing and using strengths are two different things. We need to actively commit to strengths use to increase our levels of zest!

Gratitude. As you've discovered in Week 1: Mood, there is a stack of research on the benefits of gratitude. Gratitude can be actively cultivated through a counting our blessings *Positivity Practice* or through a gratitude visit, where you write and read a letter of gratitude to someone who's made a significant impact on your life.

Love. In Week 1: Mood, we learned that love was one of the ten positive emotions. We looked at three key interventions (gratitude, kindness and forgiveness) that can have a positive impact on our relationships. These can also help build the character strength of love. For more information on cultivating love and positivity, I highly recommend Professor Barbara Fredrickson's book, Love 2.0.

Curiosity. In Week 5: Mindfulness, we'll be learning how to cultivate curiosity with a mindfulness practice. You'll discover that developing a greater level of mindfulness allows us to become more curious and psychologically flexible. As our mindful awareness grows, we begin to observe and become more curious about our thoughts, beliefs and assumptions. This increase in curiosity leads to less black and white thinking, fewer assumptions and less jumping to conclusions — all thinking traps we can fall into that negatively impact our wellbeing. You'll also be learning about these in Week 6: Mindset.

Recent research has shown that whilst these strengths continue to emerge as being highly correlated with wellbeing, there are others that make a positive impact. These include social intelligence, perseverance and humour (Martínez-Martí & Ruch, 2014).

The most important thing to remember here is that overall, knowing and using our signature strengths (no matter what they are) is positively correlated with higher levels of wellbeing.

Positivity Practice #6: Develop Your Strengths Knowledge
This week, I would like you to take the VIA character strengths assessment (either the free or paid version at www.viacharacter.org). I also want you to spend time reflecting and journalling on the questions below, which are designed to help you make the most of the assessment results. I have personally found that it can be helpful to do this outside of your usual surroundings, ideally in nature.

- What are my top five signature strengths?

- What did I learn and get out of taking the survey?

- How am I already using my character strengths at work, play and home?

- Which character strengths do I consider to be the ones most at risk of being overplayed? (Refer to the Golden Mean below).

- Which character strengths do I believe need the most development?

Strengths Use

After years of using the VIA strengths survey with individuals and groups, I have discovered that while it is great fun to identify your strengths, the greatest challenge is in putting that knowledge to use. Please reflect on the statements below to get a sense of how much you are currently playing to your strengths:

- I am regularly able to do what I do best.

- I always try to use my strengths.

- I can use my strengths in many different situations.

- I use my strengths to achieve my goals.

- My work gives me plenty of opportunities to use my strengths.

Note: Adapted from Govindji, R., & Linley, P. A. (2007). Strengths use, self-concordance and wellbeing: Implications for strengths coaching and coaching Psychologists. *International Coaching Psychology Review*, 2(2), 143-153.

The Golden Mean

Research has found value in finding a balanced expression of all your strengths (Young, Kashdan, & Macatee, 2015). This involves understanding how our strengths can:

- Work together (i.e. form a strengths constellation).

- Be developed. Research has shown that the development of lesser strengths can improve our wellbeing (Linley et al., 2010; Proyer, Gander, Wellenzohn, & Ruch, 2015).

- Be both overused and underused (Grant & Schwartz, 2011; Linley, Willars, & Biswas-Diener, 2010; Niemiec, 2014). The ideal we are aiming for is the "golden mean". In terms of strengths overuse, the "more is better" approach is not always the wisest. For example, someone with the signature strength of curiosity may not know when to stop asking questions and be accused of nosiness.

Rather than considering our lowest ranking strengths as weaknesses, it can be more helpful to think of them as "lesser strengths". It is unlikely that we would have a complete lack of any of the 24 character strengths, but there may be opportunities for development. For example, one strength that I have noticed often appears in the bottom five for many people is forgiveness. In Week 1: Mood, we learned that forgiveness is an important strength when it comes to our wellbeing. We also learned that it is possible to strengthen our forgiveness muscle.

Overall, wisdom (which has often been referred to as the "mother of all strengths") is knowing when to use the right strength, to the right amount, in the right way, at the right time.

It is important to remember:

- You can turn a strength up or down, depending on what is needed at the time.

- Avoid the "more is a better" approach or you may run the risk of turning a strength into a weakness.

- Developing a lesser strength is encouraged.

Scintillating Science

Identifying and using signature character strengths is an important pathway to a flourishing life. Individuals vary in the extent to which they use their signature strengths. A number of studies have investigated the effect of interventions intended to make participants aware of their signature strengths and to encourage them to use these strengths in their daily lives. A recent meta-analysis focused on the popular intervention "use your signature strengths in a new way" found that the signature strengths intervention had a positive impact on happiness, depression reduction, life satisfaction and flourishing (Schutte & Malouff, 2019).

Strengths Use

Once you have completed the VIA strengths assessment, it's time to put your strengths to work. While it is a lot of fun completing the survey, particularly if you do it in a team, group or family setting, there is no point knowing what your strengths are if you do not use them. This means putting your top five signature strengths to work and developing any lesser strengths you think are worth investing in.

Creating a Daily Strength Habit

- Identify a character strength you would like to use more in your life (personally or professionally).

- If you had the opportunity to use this strength for 10 minutes each day, what would you like to do more of?

- Identify a small cue (or tiny habit) that will trigger this routine. Try anchoring it to a habit you already have (such as travelling to work, turning on your computer or packing up to go home).

- Finally, identify a reward for completing the behaviour. For example, a cup of coffee or tea, ticking it off your to-do list or sharing what you've done with a buddy.

Note: Adapted from Michelle McQuaid (www.michellemcquaid.com.au).

Personally, I've used this technique to help me create a positive morning ritual. Each morning, upon waking, I practice a 10-minute mindfulness exercise (flexing my top strength of curiosity and developing my lesser strength of self-regulation). I then take 10 minutes to flex my top strength of "love of learning" by reading a brief article before I commence work for the day. I reward myself with a cup of tea as I power up the laptop.

Take a few minutes now to jot down in your journal an activity you could "anchor" a strengths-use activity to. Be sure to monitor the impact it has on your mood, energy and motivation. Noticing the positive difference will reinforce the behaviour!

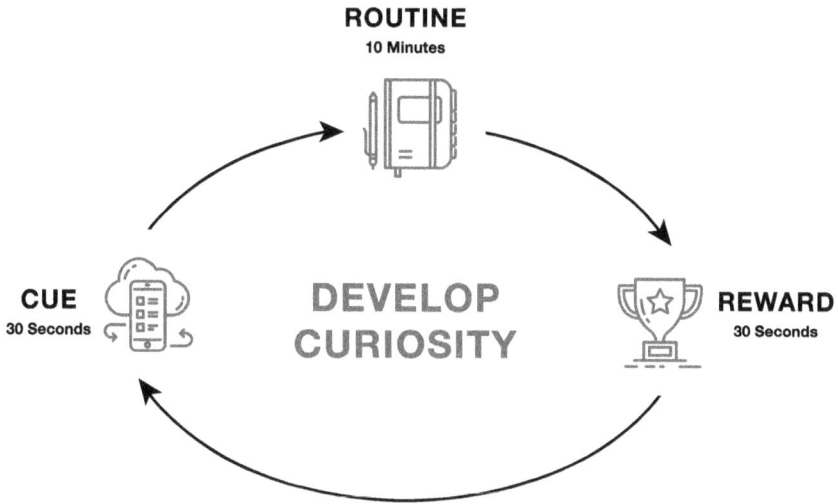

ROUTINE
10 Minutes

CUE
30 Seconds

DEVELOP CURIOSITY

REWARD
30 Seconds

Choose and Use a Lesser Strength

Another great simple activity you can do is to choose and use a "lesser strength". Over the next week please choose one of your lesser strengths and find opportunities to use it. This might involve doing a regular task in a different way or doing something completely new to you. Notice what happens and how you feel.

For example, if you choose kindness or gratitude, you could look out for an opportunity to deliberately help another person or express genuine appreciation.

Positivity Practice #7: Your Best Possible Self

Our next piece of homework for this week is imagining and creating a vision of your best possible self. The aim of this *Positivity Practice* is to write a description of you at your best that includes references to your strengths. This might include what your strengths look like in your everyday life, what others know of you based on your signature strengths and what it might look like if you developed any "lesser strengths".

This is what we refer to an as an ideal self, and the closer your current self is to your ideal self, the greater the levels of wellbeing you will experience.

This exercise is complementary to *Positivity Practice* #5: Letter from the Future.

In the Letter from the Future, you were focusing on the lived expression of your values into the future and covering all the major areas of your life such as career and relationships. The letter is externally focused; it is about how life looks on the outside.

Try to think about Your Best Possible Self exercise as being more focused on your internal world, i.e. what you're trying to create within, your inner beauty. The exercise is also an opportunity to think about your character, that is who you are, not what you do. It's the perfect exercise to bring your knowledge of your character strengths to life.

I've adapted this exercise from specific instructions used in research interventions to ensure you're more focused on your internal self (adapted from Sheldon & Lyubomirsky, 2006). Be sure to use your journal to do this exercise. Project yourself forward into the future. Imagine that you are your best (or ideal) self. Reflect on how well you are putting your character strengths to work for yourself, others and the world, how you have developed your lesser character strengths and how proud you are of the person you've become. It's important you include your values in this description of your best self. How you are living your values daily? How would you be thinking, feeling and behaving? How would others know you were at your best? Visualise yourself satisfied with who you are and how you are living your life.

Scintillating Science

Research has shown that writing expressively about yourself and your feelings has numerous benefits for health, emotional adjustment and wellbeing (Smyth, 1998). Writing about our best possible future self can enhance self-regulation (another common lesser strength) because it provides an opportunity to learn about ourselves, restructure our priorities and better understand our motives and emotional reactions (Markus & Nurius, 1986).

Success Story

Since the launch of the VIA Character Strengths Assessment in 2004, I've used the tool with a diverse range of clients, students and workshop participants. For counselling and coaching clients, the opportunity to view themselves through the lens of strengths has often led to a significant shift in how they see themselves particularly when those close to them affirm those strengths are visible on a daily basis.

Seeking feedback on our strengths can be done through a powerful exercise known as the "Reflected Best Self Exercise" (www. positiveorgs.bus.umich.edu/cpo-tools/rbse/) whereby you seek feedback (stories) from family, friends and colleagues of when they've seen you at your best. Using the language of the VIA Character Strengths can be a great way to express the strengths in action and also for the recipient to see that they are visible to those around them.

Another powerful exercise that can be done in teams or departments is to view others through the lens and language of strengths. One exercise I used each year with my students was called the "stalker task" or the "secret admirer task" and I still have so many positive memories of the impact it had. The instructions are simple - place names in a hat with each person in the group drawing a name being told to *secretly admire* (or strengths-spot) that person over a period of time (at least a month). At the end of the timeframe, when the group returns, one person stands and starts by stating who they've been "admiring" providing a short story of how they've seen that strength in action. I still recall a workshop participant who had to hold back tears when a younger member of the team genuinely gave feedback of his strengths in action. He shared with the group that he had never received such feedback his entire life. These powerful exercises provide positive feedback that is sadly often left until a eulogy is read.

Using Your Signature Strengths in New Ways

Signature strength	Suggested activity
Appreciation of beauty	• Visit an art gallery or museum and savour the experience. • Keep an excellence journal or start a regular "team excellence" meeting where you only focus on the achievement of excellence.
Authenticity	• Know your core life values and start to make small changes so you are living these values daily (see Week 2: Motivation). • Be honest about your intentions in a genuine manner.
Bravery	• Stand up for what you believe in, even when you think it might be an unpopular idea. • Speak up about the injustices you observe.
Creativity	• Enrol in a class that enhances your creativity, such as life drawing, creative writing or pottery. • Write a short workshop on a topic you are passionate about and present it to your team.
Curiosity	• Attend lectures or meetings on topics you know little about. • Ask solution-focused questions such as "What if this were to happen?"
Fairness	• Give due credit to someone you do not like. • Hear people out without interrupting.
Forgiveness	• Let a grudge go daily. • Write a forgiveness letter. Do not send it but do read it daily for a week.

Signature strength	Suggested activity
Gratitude	• At the end of the working day, write down three things you are grateful for. • Write and send a gratitude letter to a mentor.
Hope	• Write down your short- and long-term goals and make concrete plans for their accomplishment. • Find evidence for past successes and remind yourself of this when you encounter obstacles.
Humility	• For an entire day, do not speak about yourself at all. • Compliment someone on something that they do much better than you.
Humour	• Make at least one person smile or laugh per day. • Learn a "magic trick" or "party trick" and use it to surprise people.
Kindness	• Perform an anonymous favour for a teammate. • Consider ways you can show kindness to teammates who might need it.
Leadership	• Take responsibility for an unpleasant task at work and ensure it gets done. • Find ways you can show leadership in areas you never considered, such as corporate philanthropy.
Love	• Show compassion to those struggling with challenges at work. • Accept compliments without squirming and simply say "Thank you".
Love of learning	• Learn and use a new word every day. • Identify gaps in your knowledge and read a related article or book.

Signature strength	Suggested activity
Open-mindedness	• In a conversation, play the devil's advocate and take a position at odds with your private opinion. • Listen to views being expressed in team meetings with an open mind.
Perseverance	• Finish an important task at work ahead of schedule • Work for several hours without interruptions, with no telephone and emails.
Perspective	• Think of the wisest person you know and try to live one day as if you were that person. • Resolve a dispute between teammates.
Prudence	• Think twice on important decisions. Buy yourself time to consider the consequences if you need to. • Ask yourself whether your actions will be in accordance with your core values and your life goals.
Spirituality	• Daily, think about the purpose of your life. • Pray or meditate at the start of every day.
Self-regulation	• Start an exercise program and stick with it daily for a week. Find a buddy to exercise with. • Set goals and set up weekly self-coaching sessions to build your self-regulation muscle.
Social Intelligence	• Notice when a teammate does something that is difficult for them and compliment them. • When someone annoys you, understand his or her motives rather than retaliate.

Signature strength		Suggested activity
Teamwork	•	Be the best teammate you can be. Volunteer your time to a charitable group.
Zest	•	Say "Why not" three times more frequently than you say "Why?" Get enough sleep, eat a healthy breakfast and start the day with a vigorous walk.

Strengths Spotting

The third way to leverage your strengths is to start to look for strengths in others, a process referred to as strengths spotting. That might be looking for strengths in your partner, children, parents, friends or colleagues. You might suggest they also complete the VIA survey. It is easy to spot signature strengths in people you know well, so there are more benefits to looking at people you do not know well, particularly those you want to build better relationships with. Understanding others' character strengths helps us understand the contribution that others make and the benefit of increasing positive diversity. Reflect on the questions below to get a baseline on whether you are currently viewing people through the lens of strengths:

- I am able to identify people's strengths with ease.

- I get a deep sense of fulfilment from helping people to see what their strengths are.

- I always seem to know who would be the best person for the job and why.

- Spotting strengths in people makes me happy.

- Helping people understand their strengths is important to me.

Through reflecting on these questions, you will gain a sense of how you currently practice strength spotting. You will also gain a sense of how much of an emotional buzz you get from it!

Positivity Practice #8: Strengths Spotting

Your final piece of homework this week is to identify one person who you have a particularly challenging relationship with and start to view this person through the lens of strengths rather than weaknesses.

To help you do this, I suggest you review the VIA classification first and try to guess what their signature strengths might be. It might be that one of their signature strengths is being overplayed, causing you to feel irritated or envious of this strength you do not have. Either way, put on your "strengths goggles" and with a large dose of loving kindness, attempt to view this person in a different light this week.

Reflect on how you feel about this person and your relationship and how you might approach this person differently in the future now that you know more about their strengths. ✳

Week 3 Challenge Checklist

By the end of Week 3 you should have:

☐ Completed the VIA strengths survey and used the VIA reflective questions to develop strengths knowledge.

☐ Developed a daily strengths habit and/or used a lesser strength.

☐ Written your description of your best possible self, including a reference to your strengths.

☐ Have identified someone you can view through the lens of strengths

Week 4: Meaning

"The great use of life is to
spend it doing something
that will outlast it."

WILLIAM JAMES, PSYCHOLOGIST

Welcome to Week 4: Meaning, and why now more than ever, people want meaningful lives and meaningful work.

_____

We'll take a look at:

- Why meaning matters.

- How living your values creates meaning.

- Using your character strengths to create meaning.

- Creating a Personal Purpose Statement.

- Enhancing meaning at work through job crafting.

- For this week's *Positivity Practices*, you will need your list of core values (even if you don't know your top five yet) and your VIA character strengths profile.

Why Meaning Matters

Throughout history, the search for a meaningful life has led to questions such as "Who am I?" and "Why am I here?"

Humans appear to be meaning-making creatures.

Dr Viktor Frankl, a famous Austrian psychiatrist and Holocaust survivor, wrote the popular book, Man's Search for Meaning. Dr Frankl went on to develop logotherapy, a type of therapy based on meaning making, which argued that humans have a "will to meaning". He suggested that even in these dire circumstances, we attempt to find meaning and the motivation to live comes through discovering that meaning.

In the Western world, we are experiencing an over-abundance of choice, instant gratification and overly full lives, yet many still feel a sense of emptiness on the inside. Combined with the experience of living in a VUCA (volatile, uncertain, complex and ambiguous) world, these and many other factors have led to a general malaise, a sense of dissatisfaction in life and a yearning for something more. More and more people are searching for greater levels of meaning at work, where we spend at least a third of our lives, and in particular the younger generation, where many don't just want "jobs". People want work that makes a difference in the world.

This yearning and search for meaning is supported by science. Years of research tells us that people with greater levels of meaning in their lives are happier and enjoy greater wellbeing, life satisfaction and mental health. People with meaningful lives also have a greater sense of control over their lives and are more engaged in their work. Research suggests that finding a life purpose can even add years to your life! One study found that purposeful individuals lived longer than their counterparts during the 14-year period of assessment (Hill & Turiano, 2014). Who wouldn't want these benefits?

What Is Meaning?

There is currently some debate in the scientific community about what a meaningful life is. One scientific definition I resonate with is "the intrinsic value and joy a person feels when they're able to apply their strengths and values with a sense of purpose, efficacy and self-worth by contributing to society" (Baumeister & Vohs, 2002).

Most of us have an intuitive understanding of what meaning means to us. For some people, it means creating meaning in our everyday lives through our relationships and doing work that matters. For others, it's about understanding the broader purpose of our lives, such as for those who believe they have a "calling" to do the work they do.

In the scientific literature, a distinction has also been made between meaning and purpose. Simply, the suggestion is that meaning is about identifying what matters most in our everyday lives whereas purpose is about understanding the overarching aim of our lives. That is, what our lives are about and what we're here to do while we're alive on the planet.

In addition, within the scientific literature, a difference is made between the presence of meaning (whether you believe you currently have meaning in your life) and the search for meaning (the active creation of a meaningful life). Regardless of how we define it or search for it, meaning matters.

Take a moment now to reflect on what you've read. Do you currently have a sense of meaning in your life or are you searching for it? Are you more concerned with creating meaning in your everyday life or do you want to uncover your broader life purpose?

Taking some time to jot down your initial thoughts in your journal now will help you further develop your thinking as we progress through the Module. Learning and applying the science of meaning is not something to be undertaken lightly or superficially. It's important to understand that it's something that requires patience and time.

Creating Meaning

In an academic book chapter I wrote with my colleague Professor Ole Spaten from the Coaching Psychology Unit at the University of Aarlborg, Denmark, we suggested there are three primary ways of making meaning (Spaten & Green, 2018):

- **Values-based approaches**, such as values clarification, meaningful goal setting and spirituality or religion.

- **Strengths-based approaches**, such as strengths use and job crafting.

- **Vision-based approaches**, such as creating an inspirational vision or clarifying an overarching life purpose.

You've already made a start on clarifying your values, identifying your strengths and articulating your vision. You're now in good shape to apply this knowledge to the topic of meaning. It might be helpful though, before you proceed, to have those completed exercises nearby to help you connect the dots.

Values

Have you completed your *Positivity Practice* #4 from Week 2: Motivation? If not, before you continue on the topic of meaning, it is important to have given some thought to your core life values.

One of the most powerful ways to experience a sense of meaning is through living a values-congruent life. Even if you haven't identified your top five core values, take a moment to reflect on your list and asterisk the values you feel you could not live without. For example, health is a common core life value as most people value their health. Unfortunately, you often hear people lamenting about how they wished they had valued their health a little more before they got sick!

This week, you'll be investing time in identifying what matters most to you and what gives your life meaning. This will pay off big time in the long run as you begin to make values-aligned life decisions and prioritise your time according to your values.

For our first *Positivity Practice*, we will continue to hone in on your core life values and consider how well you are currently living these values.

Positivity Practice #9: Living a Values-Congruent Life

Research has shown that living a values-congruent life is associated with higher levels of psychological wellbeing. Research has also found that walking the talk (taking action on our values) is more powerful than only talking (naming our values) when it comes to our wellbeing (Sheldon & Krieger, 2014).

Many people seek counselling because of disorders such as depression, anxiety or stress, and through this exercise, they come to realise that the symptoms of these disorders, such as sleeplessness, sadness and worry, often arise as a result of not living a values-congruent life.

For some, that realisation has occurred a while back. Some people feel they are unable to live their values in an authentic way for many reasons, including letting family and friends down or having other needs that take priority over their values. The process of living values more fully is not always an easy one, but it is one that can make a significant difference to our wellbeing and lives, often over a very short timeframe.

The exercise below is something I have used for years with both clinical and coaching clients. Out of all the *Positivity Practices* I have employed over the years, this is the one that has made the biggest difference to people's wellbeing and lives.

Once you have your top five core life values, rate each value out of 5 (where 1 is not living the value at all and 5 is living the value completely). This exercise will highlight which of your values are being lived and which are not.

We can feel it in our bodies when we realise that we are saying something is important (such as our health) but we are not doing anything on a daily or weekly basis to prioritise this. We then wonder why we are languishing or not feeling great!

Top five core life values	Rating out of 5	Ideas to improve your rating

1. _____

2. _____

3. _____

4. _____

5. _____

Don't be too concerned if your rating is low. The most important thing is that you've raised your awareness around this inconsistency between "talking" and "walking". Research has also found that it can be difficult to "walk" our values, simply because life gets in the way. The continued commitment to prioritising your values and working towards our inspirational fuzzy vision (where our values are truly being lived) is still beneficial.

The next step is to ask yourself what would need to happen for you to increase your self-reported ratings on your top core life values. For example, what would you need to do this week to increase your current rating on health from a 3 to a 4? Would it be committing to three exercise sessions or booking an appointment with a dietitian to create a healthy meal plan?

Take some time to brainstorm one or two ideas for each of the values that you'd like to see a higher rating for. Also consider who could support you in doing so? While you're working towards living your values more fully in your inspirational fuzzy vision (remember your values are woven through your Letter from the Future), nothing is stopping you from living your values even a tiny bit more today, tomorrow or this week.

Many of my clients have been amazed at the impact making tiny changes towards living their values more fully can have towards feeling a greater sense of meaning in life. This includes reporting an increase in their mood and overall wellbeing in less than a week!

Strengths

Now that you are getting closer to what really matters to you from a values perspective, it is time to think about how strengths can assist you in creating greater levels of meaning in your life, not to mention help you be your most positive self. In Week 3: Might, we learned about character strengths, so please refer to your VIA character strengths survey now.

This week, we are going a little deeper into your results with a view to determining how you can create more meaning in your life by leveraging and developing strengths for yourself and others.

A sense of meaning largely comes from doing things beyond ourselves. In fact, Professor Seligman, suggests that meaning is created when we use our character strengths in service of others.

Positivity Practice #10: Using Strengths to Create a Meaningful Life

Please review your VIA strengths survey and use your journal to answer these two questions from the heart:

Which of my top five signature strengths are already helping me create meaning in my life?

Which character strengths do I want to develop to help me create more meaning in my life?

Scintillating Science

Research has found that there are three character strengths that appear to be the most important when it comes to meaning. In two studies involving people from different cultures, researchers identified curiosity, gratitude and spirituality as being key to creating a meaningful life (Peterson, Park, & Seligman, 2005; Wagner, Gander, Proyer, & Ruch, 2019). Additional strengths research has shown that two of these three (curiosity and gratitude) are more common top strengths, with research showing they are the most endorsed strengths across the globe (McGrath, 2015; Park, Peterson, & Seligman, 2006).

Take a look at where the character strengths of curiosity, gratitude and spirituality fall on your VIA survey. If they are lesser strengths, it would be in your best interest to actively work on developing them. In Week 2: Mood, you actively worked on increasing gratitude, so keep that practice up if gratitude is currently a lesser strength of yours. In Week 5: Mindfulness, you'll learn how to raise your levels of curiosity so don't worry if it's a lesser strength right now.

When it comes to spirituality, I often find this strength commonly occurring either in a client's top five or bottom five. The reason for that is currently the questions assessing this strength refer more to religion. If you do have strong religious beliefs, you're likely to have spirituality appear in your top five. If you're not a religious or spiritual person, then it's more likely this strength will appear in your bottom five. It's important to note though that spirituality doesn't necessarily mean religiousness. It refers to finding or connecting with the sacred.

Dr Ryan Niemiec, Education Director of the VIA Institute, suggests that what is sacred is unique to each person. This might include spending quality time with your family, participating in a religious ritual, observing someone else's kindness or being present to and savouring the beauty of nature. Hence meaning and the search for meaning in life fit perfectly with the strength of spirituality. If you'd like to learn more about this, visit the VIA Institute website for more information (www.viacharacter.org/character-strengths/spirituality).

Vision

In your Letter from the Future from Week 2: Motivation, you tapped into a longer-term vision of your future. Developing a vision in terms of your personal purpose is also important within the meaning-making process. To help you reflect further on the role of meaning in your life, I will ask you to write a Personal Purpose Statement. A Personal Purpose Statement provides clarity about your authentic self and gives you a sense of meaning and purpose in life. It helps define who you are and how you will live. It is an authentic guide to living a flourishing life.

Positivity Practice #11: Creating a Personal Purpose Statement
A Personal Purpose Statement can be helpful in gaining clarity as to what really matters to you and what you aim to do with your "one wild and precious life", as poet Mary Oliver writes. Regularly re-reading your Personal Purpose Statement can help you stay focused on what really matters to you, help boost your mood and bring a greater sense of meaning to your life.

Brief examples of Personal Purpose Statements:

- To honour and contribute to the positive relationships I enjoy with my family, friends and colleagues through my strengths of kindness and capacity to love and be loved.

- To find balance and peace within myself by always seeking to do what is right by using my strengths of perspective and prudence.

- To help others be their best selves and enable positive change in the world by applying my strengths of hope and persistence.

Your Personal Purpose Statement will comprise two paragraphs: what you want to do and how you will do it. The first paragraph draws on your core values and the second draws on your character strengths. Having clarified your top five core life values, now turn your values into action statements: what do you want to accomplish in life? What is your purpose? This could be to make a difference in the world or to commit to your health and wellbeing.

In the second paragraph, refer to your signature strengths and link these to your purpose. For example, your final Personal Purpose Statement could be to make a difference in the world by using your strengths of creativity, persistence and zest. Or, it could be to commit to your health and wellbeing by relying on your strengths of self-regulation and love (particularly self-love).

Use your journal to write your Personal Purpose Statement and remember to put it up somewhere visible (such as your bathroom mirror). Refer to it daily if you can and revisit it regularly to see if it still resonates with you.

Success Story

Amy was the owner of a small boutique public relations company. Amy had been in business for over ten years and was very successful. Amy was happy and proud of her success, but she felt the stories she was helping her clients tell were meaningless (at least to her). Her clients were very happy that she was increasing their sales in financial products but Amy told me she felt her work wasn't making a real difference in the world and that she wanted to use her strengths to tell a different kind of story.

We worked on clarifying Amy's values, which included helping others and making a difference. It was no surprise to Amy that she hadn't been feeling great when she realised she wasn't walking the talk, particularly when it came to making a difference.

Amy made some big decisions soon afterwards. She created a transition plan from her current client base in finance to a new client base consisting of not-for-profits and other organisations whose products and services she believed were making a significant difference in the world. She said she felt she was part of something bigger and that her strengths of creativity, curiosity and love were being utilised with more vigour than ever in her work.

Meaning at Work

A lot of research has been conducted on the development of meaning at work, although there is some ongoing academic debate as to definitions of meaning at work. Professor Michael Steger, a leading expert on the topic, suggests that the common thread across all definitions is "the idea that for work to be meaningful, an individual worker must be able to identify some personally meaningful contribution made by his or her effort" (Steger, 2017, p. 60).

In a nutshell, we need to be able to make sense out of how our work activities contribute to something greater. For some, that might be helping the company achieve its vision, and for others, it might be making meaningful connections with workmates and clients. As you will see, there are plenty of ways to create meaning at work.

When it comes to work, research tells us there are real benefits to experiencing meaningful work (Steger, 2017) and these include:

- Increased productivity.

- Increased strengths use.

- Increased career commitment.

- Increased experiences of flow at work and high-quality performance.

- High intrinsic work motivation and job satisfaction.

- Low levels of absenteeism and turnover.

When people feel engaged in meaningful work, they experience less stress and depression. For organisations, this results in less staff turnover as well as an increase in staff commitment, engagement and fulfilment. A win-win for everyone!

Job, Career or Calling?

How do you currently view your work? Research has shown that there are three primary ways to view your work: as a job, career or calling (Wrzesniewski, McCauley, Rozin, & Schwartz, 1997). Please take a moment to reflect on the three statements below and select the one that applies most to you right now.

Statement A. I work to earn enough money to support my life outside my job. If I was financially secure, I would not continue with my current line of work but would rather do something else. I cannot wait for the weekends and holidays.

Statement B. I enjoy my work but I do not expect to be in this job five years from now. I plan to move on to a better, higher-level job. I cannot wait to get a promotion.

Statement C. Work is one of the most important parts of my life. What I do for a living is a vital part of who I am. I love my work and I think it makes the world a better place.

If you have not guessed already, statement A describes a job, statement B, a career, and statement C, a calling.

Research overwhelmingly supports the fact that those who view their work as a calling (i.e. those who get a lot of meaning out of their work) report higher levels of job satisfaction and wellbeing.

Don't worry though if you resonated more with the concepts of job or career as there is nothing bad or wrong about that. The main thing to focus on is that it's important to have a sense of meaning in some way in your life. You may get your dose of meaning from your family, personal life or meaningful activities. If you are thinking you would not mind feeling a greater sense of meaning at work, read on, as we are about to look at a scientifically supported intervention designed to create more meaning at work.

Job Crafting

Job crafting is a proactive approach where employees take an active role in initiating changes to the physical, cognitive or social features of their jobs (Slemp & Vella-Brodrick, 2013).

Simply, this means employees take active charge of their jobs through adding, removing and changing their daily tasks where possible. A large part of job crafting comes down to working with our relationships at work, which play a huge role when it comes to our wellbeing. Another powerful way to craft a job is through reframing how you view your work.

Job crafters shape the boundaries that define their jobs in three main ways:

Task crafting. Job crafters change the physical or temporal boundaries around their work tasks. Task crafting consists of adding or dropping tasks, adjusting the time or effort spent on various tasks and redesigning aspects of tasks. For example, a teacher who spends time learning new classroom technology to fulfil his passion for information technology is task crafting.

Relational crafting. Job crafters redefine the relational boundaries that define the interpersonal interactions in their jobs. Relational crafting consists of creating and sustaining relationships with others at work, spending more time with preferred individuals and reducing or avoiding contact with others. For example, a marketing analyst can form a relationship with someone in sales to better understand the impact of her work on salespeople.

Cognitive crafting. Job crafters reframe the cognitive boundaries that give meaning or purpose to their tasks and relationships at work. Cognitive crafting comprises employees' efforts to perceive and interpret their tasks, relationships or job as a whole in ways that change the significance of their work. For example, a school cleaner can think of his job as enabling education by providing clean, distraction-free classrooms for students.

By positively tweaking tasks, shifting perspectives and changing relationships, you can experience different kinds of meaning from work. The good news is that job crafting can be used for the most routine jobs to the most complex and from the lowest to the highest tiers of an organisation (Berg, Wrzesniewski, & Dutton, 2010). The potential for job crafting to alter the ways in which you define the meaning of work and work identity is relevant across a broad range of job situations.

Employees are frequently presented with opportunities to make their work more engaging and fulfilling. These opportunities might be as simple as making subtle changes to your work tasks to increase enjoyment, creating opportunities to connect with more people at work or trying to view your job in a new way to make it more purposeful. While some jobs will provide more of these opportunities than others, there will be situations in all jobs where you can make subtle changes to be more engaged and fulfilled.

Below are a few suggestions for job crafting (adapted from Slemp & Vella-Brodrick, 2013). Make a note in your journal of the ones you're currently implementing or perhaps suggestions you'd like to trial at work:

- Trial new work tasks that you think better align with your values and strengths.

- Take on additional tasks at work that energise you.

- Make a connection from your role to the company's vision. How is your role helping the company fulfil its vision?

- Reflect on the ways your work has a positive impact on your life or your family's life.

- Think about how your job provides a sense of meaning or life purpose.

- Make an effort to really get to know people you work with.

- Offer to mentor someone.

Scintillating Science

In a qualitative study of employees in a variety of jobs, Berg, Grant, and Johnson (2010) investigated how employees craft their jobs in response to having unanswered occupational callings — that is, feeling drawn to pursue an occupation other than the one in which they work. They found that employees who incorporated the tasks of their unanswered callings into their current jobs experienced states of enjoyment and meaning that they associated with pursuing their unanswered callings.

For example, Jane volunteers to mentor a young person as part of her company's corporate social responsibility program. Jane believes she has a natural talent for connecting with young people and her true purpose in life is to help young people grow and develop. Her current role though is not a leadership role and it doesn't provide opportunities to work with young people. Through this volunteering role, she has an opportunity to live her unanswered occupational calling.

Overall, this research suggests that you can find meaning in many jobs. It all comes down to how creative you can be!

Positivity Practice #12: Job Crafting

In this practice, I want you to reflect on your current job and identify proactive strategies you can apply to create greater levels of meaning at work. The aim of this practice is to help you make your job more fulfilling and engaging.

Before you begin, it is important to think about your motivation for the exercise. Ask yourself, what are your motivations (underlying core values) for changing the way you do your job and approach your work? It may be to increase your levels of energy at work or to experience more joy on a daily basis. Remember, intrinsic motivation is what we are aiming for.

Use your journal to review your current role and identify small changes you could make:

Task crafting: adding and dropping tasks, adjusting time or effort spent on tasks and redesigning aspects of tasks.

Relational crafting: creating and sustaining relationships with others at work, spending more time with preferred individuals and reducing contact with others.

Cognitive crafting: reframing the way you view your role.

Note: Job crafting can be challenging and may need to become an ongoing process. You may also need the assistance of a friend, colleague, coach or counsellor. Do not feel pressured to add additional tasks to your role if this will cause stress. ❖

Success Story

When I was in my twenties, I had the worst job of my life. Before I became a Psychologist, I was a secretary — a very good one at that.

I once took a job for the wrong reasons (extrinsic reasons), for the money and for the health fund! In accepting that role, I had no say in where I would be placed and not long after taking the role I was moved to the reception of the Workers' Compensation Department in a large industrial company. Many of the employees who needed our assistance couldn't speak English well, had been injured and were angry with the circumstances they had found themselves in. The management team were very autocratic and there wasn't much joy in the office.

I decided that I wasn't going to stay in that department for very long but while I was there, I would learn all that I could, using my strengths of love of learning and curiosity, and attempt to improve the processes so that the person who took my job might find it a little easier.

I didn't realise it at the time, but I was job crafting. I made my job more meaningful through my attitude and through my actions. Less than a few months after making these changes, I was offered a much better role with a pay increase and a health fund!

Week 4 Challenge Checklist

By the end of Week 4 you should have:

☐ Identified your top five core life values (if you have not already) and assessed the extent to which you are living a values-congruent life.

☐ Identified small actions you can take this week to live your values more fully

☐ Reflected on your top five signature strengths and identified the ones you are already using to create a meaningful life as well as the ones you want to work with to create more meaning.

☐ Created a Personal Purpose Statement.

☐ Identified job-crafting strategies to create greater meaning at work.

Week 5: Mindfulness

"The most precious gift we
can offer others is our presence.
When mindfulness embraces
those we love, they will
bloom like flowers."

HICH NHAT HANH

Welcome to Week 5: Mindfulness, we will explore the important topic of mindfulness and why increasing mindfulness is non-negotiable in creating a flourishing life.

We are now coming close to completing *The Positivity Prescription*. We have focused on clarifying your values and vision and we have looked at how to leverage your strengths. We have also developed strategies to create greater motivation and meaning in your work and life.

We'll take a look at:

- What mindfulness is and why it matters.

- Determining whether you are mindful or mindless.

- Strategies for increasing mindfulness.

- Mindful relationships.

A Little Less Doing, a Little More Being

Are you with me? Are you truly here, now? Do you find your mind wandering or jumping to your to-do list?

If that's the case, it's a fairly common phenomenon as we are increasingly surrounded and bombarded by distractions in modern life. The good news is that we can learn to improve our capacity to focus and be present in the now. In fact, while this week is dedicated to mindfulness and will certainly give you the tools to improve your attentional control, the whole book or process of creating a flourishing life is underpinned by mindfulness. You'll soon discover why.

Mindfulness is very popular. It made the front cover of Time magazine in 2014 and since, interest in mindfulness has swept the world, particularly in the corporate sector and schools.

You may have read the book, *The Power of Now*, by Eckhart Tolle, which at its essence is about mindfulness. Perhaps you have read Daniel Goleman's book, *Focus*. If not, you may have read his best-selling book, *Emotional Intelligence*. What Goleman is realising, like many others in the emotional intelligence field, is that mindfulness is a powerful amplifier of emotional intelligence. It is one thing to learn the skills of emotional intelligence, but it is another to notice your emotions and mindfully respond rather than react to emotional triggers, such as people, places and situations.

While practising mindfulness, you'll learn how to find calm in our VUCA (volatile, uncertain, complex and ambiguous) world. Being mindful means paying attention to moment-by-moment experiences and observing physical sensations, thoughts and feelings (both the helpful and unhelpful ones) without suppressing or being engulfed by them.

For example, a mindful response to anger would be "This is the feeling of anger and it will pass" rather than "She makes me so angry". This is just one of the many benefits of experiencing greater levels of mindfulness.

Unless you have recently joined the growing bunch of sea changers or tree changers who've chosen a quieter life in coastal or rural areas, you are probably, like the majority of us, an urban busy bee who juggles work, relationships, family and other commitments with little time to relax.
We are really good at *doing*, not being. On the one hand, while we know from

research that striving towards meaningful life goals (i.e. doing) is associated with high levels of wellbeing, we also know that time spent just being is equally important to our wellbeing.

You might like to reflect on your ratio of doing versus being. Is it balanced towards doing, like most people? Most of us rush around in a state of constant distraction, with too many tasks we're trying to complete every day.

What Is Mindfulness?

Scientifically speaking, mindfulness is the state of being attentive to and aware of what is taking place in the present. Jon Kabat-Zinn, a pioneer in bringing mindfulness from the East to the West, defines it as "paying attention on purpose, without judgement to our experience as it unfolds moment by moment" (Kabat-Zinn, 1990).

Scientific journals and the popular press have much to say about mindfulness. However, there are a few key things to know:

- **Mindfulness is about being present in the moment.** Historically, mindfulness comes from Buddhist and other contemplative traditions, where conscious attention and awareness are actively cultivated. It is important to note though that mindfulness is not necessarily religious or specific to any religious tradition.

- **Mindfulness is an attention-training skill** in it's basic form, but it can offer us so much more in terms of enhancing our self-awareness, wellbeing, relationships and life.

- **Mindfulness is a skill that requires practice.** It is not an easy skill to acquire. Most of us are easily distracted. The challenge is learning to catch our minds wandering and to bring our focus back again and again onto whatever it is that anchors our attention. This could be our breath, an affirmation, a candle flame or anything that is a point of focus.

Let's pause now to answer three important questions:

- **What is the most important time?** That time is now.

- **Who is the most important person?** The person in front of me right now.

- **What is the most important thing to do?** To be fully present with this person and do good for them.

I love these three questions, originally from a short story by Tolstoy (1885). They are a simple reminder of the power of mindfulness and compassion. It is definitely something to bear in mind when we are in conversation with others, whether at work or home.

It's that simple: mindfulness requires us to bring our attention to whom or what is in front of us. This can help us focus on and savour the situation or person more fully. Think about your efforts to spend quality time with your family and how you can easily be drawn back to thinking about the other tasks you have to complete.

Being in the present can stop us from taking things for granted and can help us focus on the little wonders of our daily lives that give meaning to the daily grind.

Many of us spend time ruminating on the past, reflecting on things that went wrong or regretting actions we did or didn't take. This can lead to frustration, disappointment or sadness. Alternatively, many of us are future focused and put our happiness and wellbeing on hold while we strive madly towards another achievement. This is often referred to as the "I'll be happy when" syndrome.

Either way, spending too much time in the past or in the future can prevent us from being in the present and enjoying the only time we have — the time that is available to us now!

This week, I want to encourage you to stay in the present. Each time you notice your mind shifting to the past or future or onto other activities that are not related to what is currently in front of you, bring your attention back to the here and now.

Why Mindfulness?

At this point, you may be thinking this is all hippy stuff or not for you. As mentioned earlier, research on mindfulness has skyrocketed over the last 15 years, so it is difficult to argue with and well-worth considering. Research so far has provided evidence on the benefits of mindfulness in regulating our thoughts and behaviour, improving our psychological and physical wellbeing and, most importantly, improving our interpersonal relationships (Brown, Ryan, & Creswell, 2007).

Recent research has shown that mindfulness training produces a variety of wellbeing outcomes including:

Psychological and physical health (including for depression, anxiety, substance abuse, chronic pain and stress response).

Cognitive and affective processes (including for sustained attention, working memory, problem solving, positive mood and emotion regulation).

Interpersonal relationships (including for relationship quality, building perspective and pro-social behaviour).

How Mindful Are You?

Are you someone who finds it difficult to focus or who forgets someone's name as soon as you meet them, spills or drops things carelessly or arrives somewhere and wonders how you got there?

Below, you'll find a series of questions to help you determine how mindful (or mindless you are, as the case may be!) If your self-rating is low, then I strongly suggest you consider taking a mindfulness course or trial a mindfulness app. Using the 1 to 6 scale below, please rate yourself on how frequently or infrequently you currently have each experience.

1	2	3	4	5	6
Almost always	Very frequently	Somewhat frequently	Somewhat infrequently	Very infrequently	Almost Never

QUESTION	RATING
I experience physical sensations, emotions or discomfort and am not aware of them until they really grab my attention.	
I break or drop things because of carelessness, not paying attention or thinking of something else.	
I find it difficult to stay focused on what is happening in the present.	
I walk or drive to places without paying attention to what I experience along the way.	
I forget a person's name almost as soon as I have been told it.	
I run on "automatic pilot" without much awareness of what I am doing.	
I find myself listening to someone with one ear, doing something else at the same time.	
I find myself preoccupied with the future or the past.	
I snack without being aware of what I am eating.	

Adapted from: Brown, K. W., & Ryan, R. M. (2003). The benefits of being present: mindfulness and its role in psychological well-being. *Journal of Personality and Social Psychology*, 84(4), 822-848.

There is no scoring for this assessment as its overall aim is to increase your awareness of the areas where you are more or less mindful. If you answered low numbers on many questions, you are not alone. In this busy and distracted world, it is challenging to be mindful and to stay present and in the moment.

Remember, mindfulness is a skill that can be learned. I believe, as do a growing number of practitioners in my field, that these life skills should be taught more widely in schools, workplaces and communities.

Do you like a challenge? Consider downloading the 1 Giant Mind App with the free "12 Step Meditation Course" (www.1giantmind.com). The challenge involves taking 15 minutes each day for 30 days to increase your levels of mindfulness. I completed the challenge for free before I subscribed to the App.

Now, I can access a whole range of mindfulness practices that target skills such as patience and focus. A full list of mindfulness apps is available in the resources section at the back of the book.

Scintillating Science

In a study by researchers at the University of Wisconsin (Barrett et al., 2012), 149 people (aged 50 years and over) were assigned to a mindfulness-based stress reduction course, an exercise program or a control group given no particular instructions to follow. The researchers tracked how often they caught a cold or the flu over an eight-week period.

The results showed that compared to those in the control group, those who took the exercise program or mindfulness course got less sick. Those in the mindfulness group had four times fewer sick days, fewer bouts of infection and were less ill (for just over half as long), with less severe symptoms.

Depending on the year, the reduction of flu incidence and severity due to flu vaccination ranges from 13 to 70%. In comparison, cold and flu incidence, duration and severity reduction rates in the mindfulness group ranged from 14 to 60%, suggesting mindfulness meditation could be an alternative or companion to the flu vaccine.

Becoming More Mindful

While there are a number of strategies you can use to develop mindfulness, there are three key approaches I would recommend:

- Setting an intention to become a more mindful person. This intention and commitment in itself (with some gentle reminders such as a mindfulness bell, which reminds you to be mindful when the bell rings) can increase your overall levels of everyday mindfulness. I did this over 15 years ago and noticed a big difference together with a regular practice!

- Create a regular mindfulness practice. The most powerful way to increase mindfulness is to practice regularly, ideally daily. Think about it as training for your mind. Each time you bring your wandering mind back to the breath as an anchor, it is similar to lifting a weight at the gym, building your mindfulness muscle. Using an app to support you in the beginning stages of practice can be extremely helpful.

- Identify mindlessness and mindfulness triggers. Even with intention and regular practice, it is easy to slip back into mindlessness. Spend time identifying your triggers for mindlessness, such as being busy or stressed. Come up with a strategy to remind yourself of your commitment to mindfulness.

Just like creating and maintaining a regular fitness regime, a regular mindfulness practice will strengthen your attentional muscle and help you live more consciously. There are many mindfulness apps and recordings available (both free and paid), although there are benefits from attending a structured course, particularly as mindfulness practice is included as course homework and there is accountability during the course. Please refer to the resources list at the end of the book for recommendations.

Practice, Practice and Practice

We all know how important it is to practice a new skill to master it. The same logic applies to mindfulness.

You can increase your mindfulness in daily life by, first of all, focusing more on what is in front of you. For example, if you are driving your car, focus on driving the car, not talking on the phone (even if it is hands free)! You can use the activity to follow your breath and bring your attention back to the activity rather than on the hundreds of other thoughts and ideas that pop into your head.

Remember, mindfulness is the ability to bring your attention and concentration onto whatever it is you want to, when you want to! Taking a mindfulness course can also be helpful in the beginning stages as it will encourage and support you to implement a mindfulness practice, which over time becomes a routine part of your daily life.

Strong Mindfulness

Now that you've learned about your strengths, another useful way to use them is through mindfulness. That is, using your strengths to help you with your practice. Dr Ryan Niemiec, the Education Director of the VIA Institute, suggests that you can apply your own signature strengths to assist you. For example, if creativity is one of your signature strengths, you can experiment with a variety of sitting postures or try different methods for managing mind wandering.

Dr Ryan Niemiec suggests that certain strengths can be particularly helpful. If they're not your signature strengths, then it may be helpful to work on developing these:

- **Bravery** to sit with the discomfort that mindfulness so often brings.

- **Zest** can be applied in a mindfulness practice to avoid feeling lethargic or tired.

- **Perspective** can help us experience thoughts, emotions and sensations simply as temporary cognitive events.

- **Humility and humour** can help us take a lighter and less serious approach to meditation.

- **Love, kindness and forgiveness** can help us be more self-compassionate in facing the difficulties and obstacles that are so often experienced in meditation.

Mindful Relating

Research strongly supports the benefits of applying mindfulness to our relationships. Why do you think that is? Perhaps it is because we are more mindful of what is coming out of our mouths before we speak? It may also be that we are more mindful of how the other person is feeling and of the impact of what we're about to say.

This is particularly relevant right now, with the increasing recognition of unconscious (and conscious) bias and the need to be more mindful of the stereotypes we hold and the associated messages we send.

I often wonder what the world would be like if everyone's mindfulness levels went up one or two notches. My hope is that we would have a more harmonious planet with fewer arguments and accidents. It is definitely something to promote at home, school and work.

Take a moment now to consider whether there are any personal or professional relationships you would like to bring a greater level of mindfulness to. This might be with someone who presses your buttons. Imagine if you could respond mindfully rather than react mindlessly — respond rather than react! You might like to think about the best possible relationship you could have with this person. You might find that responding calmly and non-reactively might lead them to respond more positively to you, thereby improving the relationship. While we cannot change people as much as we would like to, we can always change the way we respond to them.

Positivity Practice #13: Developing a Mindfulness Practice

We all know how important it is to integrate regular exercise into our weekly timetables, but how many of us are as committed to a regular meditation practice? Using mindfulness practice in a meditative sense (i.e. spending time sitting quietly and focusing on your breath, thoughts or emotions) can greatly assist in calming the mind and enhancing psychological wellbeing.

This week, I would like you to complete at least three mindfulness meditation sessions. You might like to book-end your day with a brief mindfulness practice or decide to take a more structured approach (i.e. five times a week for 10 minutes, using a mindfulness app such as Headspace or 1GiantMind).

Whatever you decide, commitment is the key. Commitment is a strong predictor of goal success, so the higher the commitment, the better the outcome! Write down the reasons why you want to be more mindful and what the possible benefits for practising mindfulness meditation are, such as reduced stress, enhanced wellbeing and better relationships.

If you truly want to be your best possible self, a personal mindfulness practice is a key component that cannot be left out of the equation.

I have included a five-minute exercise below, adapted from a meditative practice in Matthieu Ricard's book, *Happiness: a Guide to Developing Life's Most Important Skill.* Matthieu Ricard is a French Buddhist monk often referred to as the "world's happiest man". Matthieu has undergone rigorous scientific studies to show that brain training can affect happiness. Magnetic resonance imaging (MRI) scans have shown that he and other long-term meditators experience a significant level of activity in the left pre-frontal cortex of the brain during meditation, which is associated with positive emotions and happiness. While Matthieu Ricard's abilities were far beyond those of the others involved in the trials, further studies confirmed that novices who had done relatively little meditation could increase their levels of happiness.

For this *Positivity Practice*, please sit up straight in a comfortable position. Breathe calmly for five minutes, focusing your attention on the in-and-out flow of your breath. Allow your mind to calm itself and continue to bring your attention back to your breath each time you notice your mind wandering off. Let your thoughts go and come back to the breath.

Next, bring your attention inwards, let your mind rest and cultivate a deep feeling of loving kindness and gratitude. Be mindful of the value of human existence and its potential for flourishing. Be mindful that life is short and will not last forever and of the importance of using your time wisely. Identify what truly matters in life, recall your core life values and visualise your best possible self. Visualise yourself living mindfully, lovingly and with a great appreciation of how precious life is. Resolve to live life in this way daily.

You will note the meditation above focuses on expressing loving-kindness towards others (called "metta" in Buddhism). Matthieu Ricard notes, in his *Happiness* book (p. 210), "the relationship between having a good heart and happiness is growing ever clearer. They engender and reinforce each other and both reflect oneness within our nature. Joy and satisfaction are closely tied to love and affection. As for misery, it goes hand in hand with selfishness and hostility".

Success Story

Greg was a busy professional in his fifties who worked in the financial services sector. Greg had attended one of my workshops and was surprised to see how many of his younger colleagues had spoken of their experimentation with mindfulness or other meditative practices. Many of them had learned from friends who were using it to improve their mental health and wellbeing or, alternatively, for performance in sport.

At first, Greg decided to trial it primarily to ensure he maintained a competitive edge. He trialled a few apps before he found one that worked for him. Over a six-month period, his practice was haphazard to say the least.

He eventually used an app that encouraged him to commit to a 30-day practice. This was the straw that broke the camel's back. With a consistent daily practice, at around day 22 he started to see and feel the benefits in meditation and in everyday life. He was sleeping better, being nicer to his wife and kids and was sharp at work. He started sharing his experience with his friends and family.

Everyday Mindfulness

The development of a regular mindfulness practice is essential to developing your mindfulness muscle. However, our everyday lives give us ample opportunity for practice and there are real-time benefits to everyday mindfulness.

As Thich Nhat Hanh says in his book, *The Miracle of Mindfulness*, when you are washing the dishes, make sure you are washing the dishes. This points to the need to do the opposite of what we have all been trained to do: multi-tasking. Research clearly shows that our brains do not multi-task very well. It is far better to focus on one activity at a time, both from a performance and wellbeing perspective.

While the skill of practising mindfulness in a personal practice is relatively simple, there are a few more specific skills you can use for everyday mindfulness (Linehan, 1993):

- **"What" skills.** Observing, noting and labelling events, thoughts and emotions and entering fully into them.

- **"How" skills.** Taking a no-judgement approach, focusing on one thing in the moment and being effective (i.e. doing what is needed rather than worrying about what is right or second-guessing the situation).

Positivity Practice #14: Creating an Everyday Mindfulness Ritual
In *The Miracle of Mindfulness*, Thich Nhat Hanh recommends a number of everyday mindfulness exercises. I have included some of these below but be sure to pick up a copy of his book or audiobook. I've also included tips from Headspace (www.headspace.com) who have fabulous videos and blogs on making mindfulness part of your daily life.

Pick one activity to practice this week:

- **Mindfulness while listening to music.** Breathe long and deep breaths. Do not get lost in the music, rather, experience it fully and practice mastering your breath.

- **Mindfulness while in conversation.** Breathe long and deep breaths. Listen to a friend's words and to your replies. Do not jump ahead to thinking of what you will say next. Rather, be present in the conversation and listen. Reflect back what you have heard. Practise mastering your breath during the conversation.

- **Mindfulness while making tea, washing dishes, cleaning the house, brushing your teeth or taking a shower or bath.** In all these activities, allow time for the activity, move three times slower than usual, fully focus your attention on each task and maintain mindfulness of your breath, particularly when your thoughts wander.

- **Mindfulness upon waking.** Write the word "smile" on a post-it stuck on the ceiling or wall so that it is the first thing you see upon waking. Use this time to focus on your breath and to drop into yourself. Inhale and exhale three breaths while maintaining a half-smile.

- **Mindfulness when irritated.** If someone does something to annoy or irritate you, give a half-smile. Inhale and exhale quietly and maintain the half-smile for three breaths.

- **Mindfulness while waiting in line.** Rather than scrolling through Instagram or checking emails, use the time to practice mindful breathing and mindful awareness of your posture and internal emotional state.

- **Mindful colouring.** Choose one of the many mindful colouring books available for purchase now. Focus on how you're holding the pencil, the colours you are using and the act of colouring in between the lines.

- **Be mindful of the effects of these exercises.** If you notice the benefits to you and to those around you, you will be more likely to keep them up due to positive reinforcement.

Stop

Take A Breath

Observe

Proceed

The STOP Technique

Another simple technique you might like to trial is the STOP technique developed by Professor Jon Kabat-Zinn. There may be times during the day when you're so busy you're not aware of what's happening inside you. You may be so dedicated to getting the task done that you don't prioritise anything else, such as taking a moment to be aware of yourself and your needs. This approach to life is not sustainable.

The exercise, summarised by the acronym STOP, is an informal way of practising everyday mindfulness to help alleviate stress and anxiety in daily life. The STOP exercise is also helpful in relieving physical sensations such as tense shoulders, a clenched jaw, tension in the body, hunger, fatigue or the need for a break.

Take two to five minutes to **Stop** what you're doing and try to sit or stand as still as possible, limiting movement as much as possible.

Take a couple of deep breaths from your diaphragm. Breathe in for four seconds, hold for two to three seconds and breathe out for four seconds. You may choose to repeat this several times.

Observe what's happening inside your body and mind, notice the thoughts you're having or have had over the past several minutes prior to stopping. Observe what you're feeling and where those feelings are located in your body (i.e. if you identify that you feel frustrated or stressed, where in the body are you feeling the stress?). Can you notice what thoughts are contributing to the feeling?

Then, **proceed** with whatever you were doing prior to stopping. Try to move on to your activity with more awareness.

To reinforce your mindfulness practice, you can:

- Practise this exercise anytime you feel tense or upset.

- Practise before or after certain activities (at work or home).

- Schedule reminders in your mobile phone to remind you to STOP and check in.

- Aim to do this exercise around three times per day (i.e. in the morning, at lunchtime and in the afternoon) for at least five minutes each time. ✼

Week 5 Challenge Checklist

By the end of Week 5 you should have:

☐ Raised your awareness of how mindful (or mindless) you are.

☐ Completed at least three mindfulness practices.

☐ Identified at least one everyday mindfulness ritual to trial to increase your levels of mindfulness.

☐ Practised the STOP technique on a daily basis.

Week 6: Mindset

"There is nothing either good or bad but thinking makes it so."

WILLIAM SHAKESPEARE

Welcome to Week 6: Mindset, the final week of the program. Mindset is key to sustaining the positive changes you have made during the program.

In this concluding week, we will look at:

- What mindset is.

- Fixed, growth and benefit mindsets.

- How to think more optimistically.

- Catching your automatic negative thoughts.

- Creating performance-enhancing thoughts for success.

What Is a Mindset?

Mindsets are our beliefs about ourselves, others and the world. They have also been defined as the beliefs (conscious and unconscious) that we hold about the changeability of our talents, intelligence and character (Dweck, 2006).

Most of us realise that when it comes to mindsets and their associated thought patterns, the negative often outweighs the positive in everyday life, particularly if our mood is low.

As we've learned, humans have a negativity bias, where we pay more attention to and give more weight to the negative rather than the positive, particularly when avoiding a loss (Rozin & Royzman, 2001; Sparks & Ledgerwood, 2017).

Our mindsets are largely developed through our early childhood experiences. Our core beliefs are shaped by the messages we are given by parents and significant others, and we often carry these beliefs and mindsets unconsciously into adulthood. While some of these beliefs are helpful, many are not. It's often not until adulthood that we begin to question these mindsets and actively work on changing them if we realise they're having a negative impact on our life.

Working with people's mindsets has been the bread and butter of Psychologists for decades. It is often these unhelpful and (more often than not) irrational thoughts that get the better of us, particularly when we are stressed or suffering. Historically, you would not have done anything to address these unhelpful mindsets and thinking patterns until things went bad. In many cases, it was these thinking patterns that led to depression, anxiety and other relationship, career or life challenges.

At this point in time, most people in our community are blissfully ignorant to the powerful role mindsets have on their lives. People often believe it is impossible to change their mindset. My hope with this program is that more people become proactive about their mindsets and learn mindset skills they can use when things get difficult. In fact, kids are learning these skills at school to help them face challenges in our fast-paced and ever-changing world.

Fixed Versus Growth Mindsets

A popular way to look at mindsets is through the pioneering work of Professor Carol Dweck from Stanford University. Professor Dweck's research has found that there are two primary mindsets: fixed versus growth. People with fixed mindsets believe "they are the way they are" and that their talents and intelligence are cast in stone. They avoid challenges and stick to what they know they can do well. As a result, their beliefs prevent their growth and development.

People with growth mindsets, on the other hand, believe their talents can be developed and that they can improve over time. They believe their brain is like a muscle that can be developed with use, leading to the desire to improve. They embrace challenges and life's obstacles do not discourage them. They see failure as an opportunity to learn. Effort is seen not as something to avoid, but as necessary for growth and development. Criticism and feedback are viewed as useful sources of information.

By acknowledging the two mindsets, you can start thinking and behaving in new ways. You can take an online assessment to determine whether you hold a fixed or growth mindset (www.sparqtools.org/mobility-measure/growth-mindset-scale).

Do not be overly concerned if you think you have a fixed mindset before taking the test. The good news is that you can develop and shift your mindset through effort and practice as demonstrated by neuroscientific research, i.e. neuroplasticity.

It's important to understand though that nobody has a growth mindset in everything all of the time. Professor Dweck has suggested that we each have a mix of fixed and growth mindsets. You might have a growth mindset in one area, topic or skill but taking on a challenge that pushes you outside of your comfort zone can trigger a fixed mindset, for example when you encounter someone who is better than you at something. It's about understanding when and why our fixed mindsets are triggered.

In addition, while it can be quite liberating to understand that it is possible to change your brain and your mindset, it might not be easy or quick! Changing your mindset will take some practice but I will be sharing a powerful strategy that is as simple as learning your ABCs.

Benefit Mindset

Dweck's work on mindset has been extended beyond its traditional focus on learning and accomplishment to what's referred to as the benefit mindset (Buchanan & Kern, 2017). The authors suggest that a global interest in wellbeing is emerging (Rusk & Waters, 2013), which encompasses both being well and doing good.

The benefit mindset therefore focuses on not only being the best in the world, but being the best *for* the world. This approach encompasses both individual and collective perspectives and is oriented towards collectively creating the future. This approach to mindset highlights not just what and how we do things, and the associated mindsets we bring, but why we do things. The benefit mindset asks us to cultivate a willingness to work collectively, accessing a deeper level of our humanity (Heifetz, Grashow, & Linsky, 2009; Scharmer & Kaufer, 2013).

The benefit mindset connects beautifully to the concept of meaning, which we focused on in Week 4: Meaning. As you'll discover, meaning making is often concerned with our relationships and is connected to something bigger than or beyond ourselves (transcendence). Developing a benefit mindset helps us flourish not in isolation but as partners in each other's flourishing.

Fixed MINDSET	Growth MINDSET	Benefit MINDSET
Everyday experts who seek perfection and avoid failure	**Everyday learners** who seek growth and development	**Everyday leaders** who seek to 'be well' and 'do good'
Focus on reproducing **what** they know	Focus on improving **how** they do what they do	Focus purposefully on **why** they do what they do
Believes their strengths are innate gifts that can't be developed and focus on **perfecting** **their abilities.**	Belives their strengths can be developed with effort, reaching **higher** **levels of achievement** and ability.	Believes in developing their strengths and **meaningfully contributes** to a future of greater possibility.

Success Story

In my twenties, I struggled with a fixed mindset. I had left school early with no intention to attend university. I didn't think I was smart. With encouragement and challenge from my family and friends, I began to develop a growth mindset.

As I received positive feedback on my essays and exams, I gained more evidence that I was more than capable of learning, and in fact I was excelling in my studies. The active development of a growth mindset didn't stop as I had to continually challenge my automatic negative thoughts (ANTS) throughout my career. However, I began to see myself as having a growth mindset, which has helped me take on a multitude of challenges both at work and in life.

A few years back, I decided to learn French virtually with a French teacher. Halfway through my first lesson, I became aware of a barrage of ANTS: "What are you thinking? You're too old to learn another language! Don't you know the research says it's much easier to learn a language when you're a child?" I had to draw on all of my skills to overcome these ANTS, which included the development of performance-enhancing thoughts (PETS) such as "Suzy, one of your top strengths is love of learning, so focus on the enjoyment of learning, not on being perfect. There are many examples of people who have learned another language as an adult. Of course you can do it!"

I completed the course and whilst I didn't become fluent, I was able to order breakfast, lunch and dinner on my trip to France.

Optimism Versus Pessimism

There has been over 20 years of research on optimism as a psychological construct, which has shown that the benefits of being optimistic include better health, a longer and happier life, less stress and anxiety, a successful career, better relationships and more resilience. On the other hand, the costs of being pessimistic include increased risk of depression, earlier death, inertia in the face of adversity, a lower immune system, poor performance at work, poor relationships and ill-health in the physical and mental domains.

Within Positive Psychology, optimism as a style of thinking has pride of place. Optimistic thinking is a key approach to positivity, wellbeing, resilience and personal growth.

Scientifically, there are two discussions on optimism. One has to do with what is known as dispositional optimism, viewed as an inherent part of being human that developed through the evolution of the human species. This type of optimism reflects the global expectation that good things will be plentiful in the future and bad things scarce. Theory suggests that there are individual differences in optimism, which explains why some of us reside at one end of the optimism-pessimism spectrum.

Being optimistic involves thinking positively about our goals and having positive expectations for future events. When obstacles occur in the pursuit of goals, optimists persist, whereas pessimists give up. You can take a free measure of your own dispositional optimism by undertaking an optimism test (www.authentichappiness.org).

Another body of research on optimism has been conducted by Professor Seligman and colleagues. Before launching the field of Positive Psychology, Seligman started his early career researching the effects of learned helplessness and then developed the theory of learned optimism. Much research has been conducted on optimism and its association with positive mood, good morale, perseverance and effective problem solving (Peterson & Steen, 2009).

Seligman's and his colleagues' approach to optimism explores what is known as *explanatory style*, that is, how we explain the causes of adversity or bad events (Buchanan & Seligman, 1995). Optimists explain bad events as external (i.e. not their fault), unstable (i.e. not long-lasting) and specific (i.e. a one-off event). On the other hand, pessimists view bad events as internal (i.e. their fault), stable (i.e. long-lasting) and global (i.e. occurring across many situations). For example, when John was fired, he thought "I stuffed up *(internal)*, I'll never get another chance like that *(long-lasting)* and everything is hopeless *(global)*". Jim, on the other hand, thought "Damn cutbacks *(external)*, a bit of bad luck *(short-term)* but I have learned many skills that will be an asset to my future employer *(one-off)*".

These contrasting interpretations are termed permanence, pervasiveness and personalisation (the three Ps):

* **Permanence.** When something goes wrong once, a pessimist will believe that it will always go wrong. An optimist will believe they can ensure they can perform better next time and that the challenge was just a temporary setback.

* **Pervasiveness.** For pessimists, when things go wrong, they catastrophise. They see failures as pervasive across all situations and often conclude they are a total failure. For optimists, when things go wrong, they view it as a specific setback in a specific situation, rather than affecting things globally.

* **Personal.** Pessimists blame themselves when things go wrong and they internalise the problem. They often do not look for evidence to the contrary or other variables that may have come into play. Optimists tend to look outside of themselves for the answers as to why things went wrong, such as external events that may have been outside their control.

Recent studies of cancer patients have shown that optimists are more likely to engage in active attempts to deal with the stress of cancer and its treatment through an optimistic explanatory style. Optimists are less likely to dwell on negative emotional experiences and do not employ avoidance strategies or disengage from active coping.

Research has also shown that optimistic thinking can prevent depression. As such, cultivating optimism is something you may want to consider for yourself, your family and children.

Scintillating Science

In a study testing whether the relationship between exercise and health is affected by people's mindsets, researchers measured how exercise affected the physiological health of 84 female cleaners working in hotels.

In the experimental condition (the informed group), the cleaners were told that the work they do (cleaning hotel rooms) is good exercise and satisfies the national recommendations for an active lifestyle. They were provided with examples of how their work was in fact great exercise. Subjects in the control group were not given this information.

Although the cleaners' behaviour didn't change, nor the amount of exercise they were doing, four weeks after the intervention, the informed group perceived themselves to be getting significantly more exercise than before. As a result, compared with the control group, they showed a decrease in weight, blood pressure, body fat, waist-to-hip ratio and body mass index. These results support the hypothesis that health is significantly affected by mindset.

Learning to Be More Optimistic

If in Week 1: Mood, you assessed yourself as languishing, then this module can make a big difference to your mood and life. It is a great opportunity to identify whether certain types of mindsets or thinking patterns are significantly impacting your mood.

While clinical depression sometimes requires the use of medication (please discuss this with your General Practitioner), there are proven practical psychological strategies, including learning to be optimistic, that you can use to pull yourself out of a bad mood. As we all know, a bad mood at the beginning of the day ("getting out of the wrong side of the bed") can set the mood for the whole day.

In psychology, there has been an enormous amount of research conducted on the effectiveness of psychological treatments for depression. These include cognitive behavioural therapy (Beck, 1967) and rational-emotive therapy (Ellis, 1957). More recently, many self-help books have provided practical strategies for changing your thinking to help improve your mood. One of the best evidence-based books I recommend is *Change Your Thinking* by Dr Sarah Edelman.

The basic idea of cognitive behavioural therapy is that our emotions and behaviours are not triggered by events themselves but by how we interpret those events. Professor Seligman suggests that by using the ABCDE model (adapted from Ellis & Dryden, 1987), we can better understand our thoughts, emotions and behaviours to think more optimistically and build resilience for the future.

Learning Your ABCs

The ABCDE model suggests that when we experience adversity (A), ranging from daily hassles to life-changing events, we develop beliefs (B) around why things happened (events and circumstances and our role in them). Leading on from this belief are emotional and behavioural consequences (C). To overcome these unhelpful or irrational beliefs, we can dispute (D) our beliefs, which energises us and leads to a more effective and energising (E) outcome.

```
┌─────────────┐      ┌─────────────┐      ┌─────────────┐
│      A      │ ───► │      B      │ ───► │      C      │
│             │      │             │      │             │
│ Activating  │      │ Beliefs about│     │The emotional│
│  Event or   │      │  Event or   │      │and behavioural│
│  Adversity  │      │  Adversity  │      │consequences │
└─────────────┘      └─────────────┘      └─────────────┘
                                                  │
                                                  ▼
        ┌─────────────┐      ┌─────────────┐
        │      E      │ ◄─── │      D      │
        │             │      │             │
        │Effective new│      │ Disputations│
        │beliefs replace│    │ to challenge│
        │the irrational ones│ │irrational beliefs│
        └─────────────┘      └─────────────┘
```

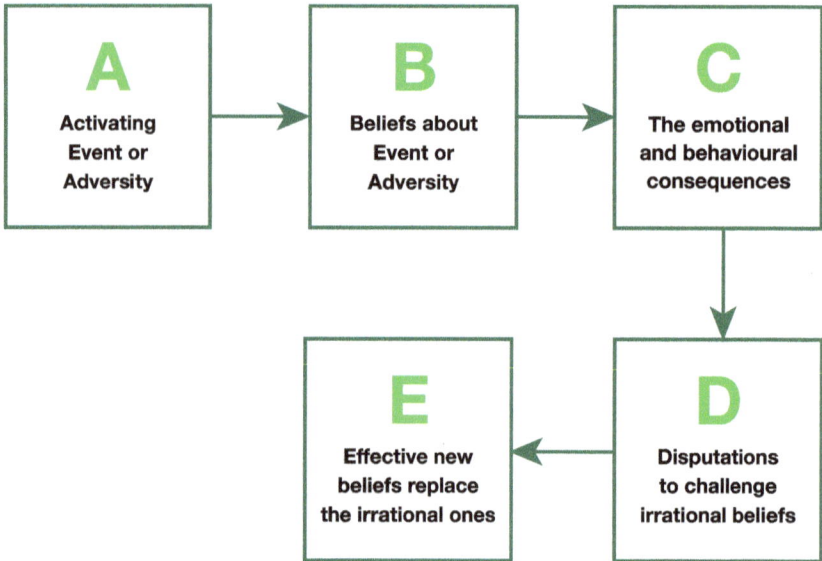

Let's say that this morning, your alarm didn't go off, you missed your bus and you were late for an important meeting that your boss had requested you attend. In this situation, your ABCDEs would be:

- **Activating Event.** Waking up late, missing the bus and being late for the meeting.

- **Beliefs.** "My boss is going to kill me, I may as well not turn up for work. Maybe I should call in sick? I will probably lose my job, which means I won't be able to pay my mortgage. I will be homeless and sleeping on the street!"

- **Consequence.** You turn up late, flustered, unable to think clearly and unable to have any sensible input during the meeting.

- **Disputation.** Ask yourself, "What is the worst that could realistically happen?" Ask yourself what options you have, such as catastrophising and creating the outcome you are fearing versus moving into a solution-focused mindset and identifying ways you could make it to the meeting. How could you explain what happened to your boss?

- **Effect.** Decide on a solution and act on it, feeling more optimistic about the outcome.

Positivity Practice #15: Change Your Thinking with ABCDE

This week, I would like you to use the ABCDE Positivity Practice below to work through a common challenge you have at work or home.

- **Adversity.** These are situations that push your buttons. These might include juggling work-life balance, multi-tasking, conflict situations or dealing with others' negative emotions. Take some time this week to identify your high-risk situations where you are more likely to react with strong emotions. You might notice some themes occurring and this can be a great insight into yourself.

- **Beliefs.** Refer to one of the situations you have noted above and recall that situation in your mind in as much detail as possible. Try to identify what sort of thoughts were going through your mind, such as "Who do they think they are!" These thoughts can be referred to as automatic negative thoughts (ANTS). ANTS are negative, unhelpful and occur very quickly. We are often unaware that we have ANTS as we may only notice an emotion, such as anger.

- **Consequence.** This includes the effect ANTS have on your mood and the behaviours that follow. For example, you could have a road-rage outburst when someone cuts you off in traffic, feeling angry and shouting at the driver.

- **Disputation.** ANTS are often irrational and at the very least unhelpful. The next step is to look for evidence to dispute your ANTS and to generate alternative thoughts and beliefs. For example, "I haven't done anything productive all year!" Ask yourself whether that statement is 100% true.

What evidence could you find to dispute it or support the fact that you have achieved something? What new perspective could you take to help you think and feel differently, such as "I've taken useful steps towards my goals and feel confident to take the next step".

Refer to the disputation questions below to help you dispute your ANTS:

- **Evidence.** Are the negative beliefs factually incorrect? Ask, what is the evidence for this belief?

- **Alternatives.** Are there alternative ways to look at the problem that are less damaging to yourself and may help you feel more hopeful about the situation?

- **Implications.** Is the outcome really as bad as you think? Learn to de-catastrophise.

- **Usefulness.** Are your beliefs useful or helpful? It can be helpful to realise that even negative situations can work out in the long run.

- Finally, in the **Effect** phase of the ABCDE practice, you can assess the result of changing your thinking. How do you feel now that you have a new perspective on things? You may feel quite different from how you felt initially.

Remember, being optimistic is a skill. It takes practice, practice and practice to apply your ABCDEs successfully. You can use the journal prompts below to guide you through your practice:

- **Adversity.** What is the situation you are facing?

- **Beliefs.** What are your thoughts about it?

- **Consequence.** What are the outcomes of these thoughts?

- **Disputation.** How else could you think about this situation?

- **Effect.** What is the alternative preferred outcome?

Can You Be Too Optimistic?

There are times when the consequences of things going wrong are significant. As such, it is worth considering pessimistic outcomes and choosing the prudent or cautious route. An example is being tempted to buy a house you cannot afford. Your salary may increase and you may be able to meet the repayments. But what if this doesn't happen?

There are benefits in learning to be a defensive pessimist, particularly if you are a rose-coloured optimist. Personally, as a cheerful and optimistic person, this is something I have had to learn and apply. Engaging in what is known as defensive pessimism (Norem & Chang, 2002) allows us to work through worst-case scenarios to plan strategies and move from planning to doing. For some people, these strategies are most effective when they anticipate the worst and plan to minimise disastrous outcomes.

When to use optimism	When to use defensive pessimism
In a challenging situation.	If your goal is to plan for a risky and uncertain future.
If you want to improve your mood and find solutions.	When the cost of failure is high.
If the situation is likely to be long-winded and your physical health is an issue.	When counselling others whose future is dim.

Can you think of situations in your personal life when you could use optimism or defensive pessimism? Reflect in your journal now.

Catching ANTS

Doing the *Positivity Practice* may have raised your awareness of your current mindset and thinking patterns. Do your thoughts help or hinder you in daily life? If you are like most of us, you will have experienced many ANTS.

At their worst, ANTS are irrational, where we jump to conclusions, make unfounded assumptions and believe we know what others are thinking. For example, many of us catastrophise and turn everything into a disaster, when in fact things may not be as bad as we think.

Through decades of research, Psychologists have identified certain types of ANTS or common thinking traps. For example, in depression, people usually think that everything is hopeless and that things will never improve.

When we get angry, we often have a lot of "shoulds", such as "He shouldn't have done that!" While that may be true to some extent, situations don't always turn out the way we expect and holding on to these "shoulds" leaves us irritated, frustrated and disappointed.

When we are fearful, we have a lot of "what ifs", such as "What if I embarrass myself in front of my team?" Most often, these fears never materialise. Remember that FEAR stands for false evidence appearing real.

Below, you will find a set of common thinking traps. As you reflect on the list, asterisk the ones that are relevant to you. Learning skills to catch and manage these thinking traps is crucial to a flourishing life. Once you begin to become aware of your trigger situations, you start to realise just how powerful ANTS can be. Challenging those thoughts takes practice.

Common Thinking Traps

All-or-nothing thinking. There are no shades of grey. If your performance is not perfect, you view yourself as a complete failure.

Overgeneralisation. One negative event is viewed as an endless pattern of defeat.

Disqualifying the positive. You discount all positive experiences.

Jumping to conclusions. You make negative interpretations that are not supported by evidence. You feel that you know what other people think of you. You make negative predictions and you are certain they will come true.

Magnification or minimisation. You exaggerate the importance of an error or someone else's achievements. You underrate your strengths or someone else's weaknesses.

Emotional reasoning. You believe that your emotions mirror reality ("I feel it, so it must be true").

Labelling and mislabelling. You label yourself inappropriately ("I'm a loser"). You label others wrongly ("He's a stupid idiot").

Personalisation. You blame yourself for a negative external event for which you were not responsible. For example, a friend becomes sick and calls you to cancel a dinner date. You blame yourself for the cancellation.

Positivity Practice #16: Catching ANTS
The aim of this practice is to identify common thinking traps and associated ANTS you regularly fall into. Most people will find they engage in one or two thinking errors more than the others. I have also had clients tell me that once they start monitoring ANTS, they have more ANTS than ever! This is not the case, but monitoring them makes you more aware of them.

At this stage, being aware of ANTS and the powerful impact they can have on your mood and behaviours is a good start. While techniques such as cognitive behavioural therapy or rational-emotive therapy require you to challenge and replace these ANTS, a newer approach gaining much evidence is acceptance and commitment therapy or training (commonly referred to as ACT; Hayes, Strosahl, & Wilson, 1999).

ACT recommends being mindful of ANTS without buying into evaluative and judgemental language. This involves practising being an observer of your ANTS, watching your thoughts like leaves floating along a stream and moving in a values congruent direction. Hence the importance of knowing and living your values! If you want to learn more about ACT, I can highly recommend Dr Russ Harris's book, *The Happiness Trap*.

When it comes to your emotions, Jack Kornfield, a Psychologist and Buddhist monk, in his book, *A Path with Heart*, suggests an activity called name your demons, where you simply name the emotion repeatedly (such as anger, anger, anger) until it loses its power and impact.

Creating PETS for Success

While you will be using the ABCDE method to help you this week, another very simple strategy to overcome ANTS is to turn them into your PETS!

PETS stand for performance-enhancing thoughts. PETS are not positive thinking. They need to be based on evidence and reality. As we've discovered earlier, our ANTS are often irrational, so creating PETS is often simply a case of searching for evidence that contradicts our ANTS, which leads to a more realistic and helpful way of thinking about the situation. You can use PETS for yourself, which are much like affirmations, and you can use them in regard to people and situations you are facing.

PETS as thoughts can help shift our deeper beliefs over time. PETS can help us perform better (in academic, sports or competitive settings) and they can help us become the person we want to be. For example, repeating PETS in regard to how you want to view yourself can shift your self-concept over time. There are two main ways you can use PETS. Firstly, you can use PETS to replace your ANTS. At first, this won't happen in real-time but using the ABCDE *Positivity Practice* over time, you'll get better at this and eventually be able to execute this skill like a mental gymnast!

Secondly, you can create PETS to support a goal you are working towards or create PETS to support you in becoming your best possible self (remember *Positivity Practice* #7 in Module 3: Might).

ANTS	PETS
"I'll never be able to do this. I have so many ANTS. I think I have an ANT farm!"	"I know it's not going to be easy to change a mindset I've held for years and replace my ANTS with PETS, but I'm committed and determined to learn this skill. If I find it too challenging to learn by myself, I'll seek professional help to master this skill."
"I just don't have it in me be a more forgiving person."	"Over time and with a growth mindset, I can learn to be more forgiving. I know it's ultimately going to help me feel better, physically and mentally."
"I never achieve the goals I set for myself or complete programs I sign up for."	"I'm going to do everything within my control to set myself up for success. I have many strengths I can draw on. This time things are different, so I'm increasing my chances of success."

Positivity Practice #17: Creating Friendly PETS

In this practice, I would like you to create three PETS to support your continued commitment to your wellbeing. For example, this could be "I have made such great progress and I am committed to following through and will seek additional support if needed".

Use your journal to do this exercise and be sure to create positive visual primes to ensure these PETS become your new way of thinking. I usually write my affirmations in lipstick on the mirror. You can also write them on colourful post-it notes and put them in places where they will be highly visible. ❖

Week 6 Challenge Checklist

By the end of Week 6 you should have:

- [ ] Have a better understanding of how mindsets influence your life.

- [ ] Know the difference between a fixed mindset, a growth mindset and a benefit mindset.

- [ ] Applied the ABCDE model to a current life challenge.

- [ ] Be more mindful of your ANTS and thinking traps.

- [ ] Have created three PETS for ongoing success.

Conclusion

"Come to the edge," she said.
"We can't, we're afraid!" they responded.
"Come to the edge," she said.
"We can't, we will fall!" they responded.
"Come to the edge," she said.
And so they came.
And she pushed them.
And they flew."

GUILLAUME APOLLINAIRE

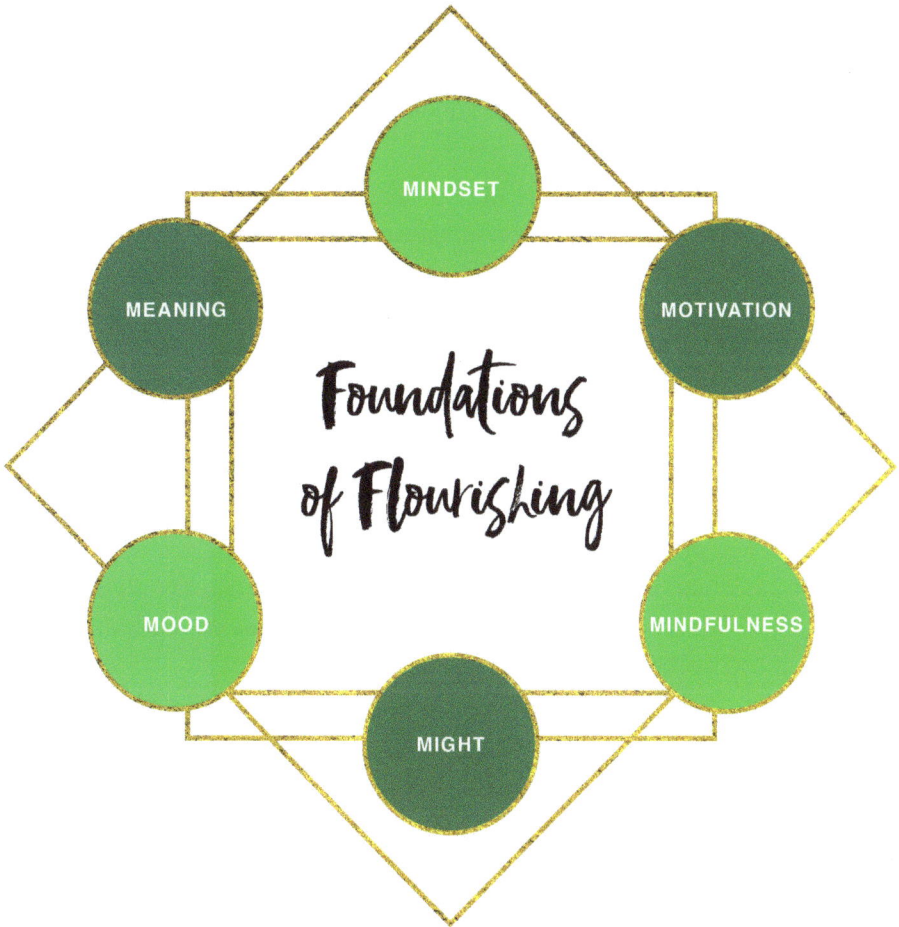

Foundations of Flourishing

- MINDSET
- MOTIVATION
- MINDFULNESS
- MIGHT
- MOOD
- MEANING

Well done, you made it through to the end of *The Positivity Prescription*. Well, it's not really the end, in fact, it's just the beginning! The greatest challenge for you now is to continue down this path to positivity and sustain the positive changes you've created.

In this final Module, we will:

- Review the six components of *The Positivity Prescription* and reminisce on all the good stuff you have learned and applied.

- Reflect on what worked well and the wins you have experienced.

- Commit to goals and determine the next steps to sustain your positivity, wellbeing, being your best self and living your best life.

Looking Back

In the introduction Module, I gave you a broad overview of *The Positivity Prescription* and its core components. I also highlighted the importance of completing the *Positivity Practices* and using a journal to track your progress and light-bulb moments.

I would like to encourage you to continue to use your journal, as regularly using a journal will allow you to build your levels of self-awareness and support you in creating and sustaining the changes you desire.

Personally, I've journalled for over 20 years and it's been amazing to see the evolution of my self-awareness and self-management. The journals have helped me when I didn't have anyone available at the time to talk to and when I chose to consult my own "wise self".

At the beginning of our journey, I encouraged you to get a coach, whether that be a professional or a buddy. Please consider trialling a professional coach if you have never had one (email us at info@thepositivityinstitute.com.au for details on our own virtual Positive Psychology Coaching packages). There is nothing like accountability and support to help you see your goals through to success!

If that isn't for you, you can set up a co-coaching arrangement with a like-minded buddy or schedule in a weekly self-coaching session with yourself. I'll come back to this important point later in this Module.

Let's do some positive reminiscing now (another mood-boosting strategy) and review the six steps to positivity.

Week 1: Mood

In Week 1: Mood, we looked at how both negative and positive emotions are important for our wellbeing. I highlighted the need to seek professional support if you have difficulties managing your negative emotions, where fear becomes anxiety or a phobia, or sadness becomes clinical depression.

We also talked about how it wasn't until the emergence of Positive Psychology that the study of positive emotions really took off. Now, we can prescribe mood-boosting activities that are scientifically proven to enhance your wellbeing, such as in *The Positivity Prescription*. In Week 1: Mood, we focused in on gratitude, kindness and forgiveness interventions.

Week 2: Motivation

In Week 2: Motivation, you identified your readiness and reasons for change and we highlighted the importance of intrinsic motivation. We also explored how your values and vision drive intrinsic motivation. You identified your top five core life values and wrote your Letter from the Future.

Week 3: Might

In Week 3: Might, we spent time reviewing your character strengths and the role they play in helping you be your best possible self and creating your best possible life. I asked you to consider how you can leverage your signature strengths. I also asked you to identify which of your lesser strengths might need further development, such as forgiveness or gratitude. I also asked you to start viewing people through the lens of strengths (strength-spotting).

Week 4: Meaning

In Week 4: Meaning, we considered the role meaning plays in our wellbeing, particularly at work. You created a Personal Purpose Statement to help you stay focused on what really matters. You were introduced to the concept of job crafting and may have made small or big changes to your job to experience more meaning and joy at work.

Week 5: Mindfulness

In Week 5: Mindfulness, we reviewed the benefits of being mindful of the present rather than ruminating on what happened in the past or worrying about the future. We also looked at how important it is to engage in a regular mindfulness practice and daily mindfulness activities.

Week 6: Mindset

In Week 6: Mindset, we highlighted the importance of adopting a growth and/ or benefit mindset and learned about common thinking traps. You used the ABCDE model to experience more optimism. We also spent time catching our automatic negative thoughts (ANTS) and turning them into performance-enhancing thoughts (PETS).

Scintillating Science

Savouring is the ability to be aware of positive experiences and regulating positive feelings about such experiences. Savouring can include luxuriating (e.g. easing into a hot bath), marvelling (e.g. at a Santorini sunset), basking (e.g. positively reminiscing on past achievements) and thanksgiving (e.g. expressing gratitude for all the good in our life).

Professors Fred Bryant and Joseph Veroff, pioneers in the scientific study of savouring, suggest it is more than pleasure — it also involves mindfulness and "conscious attention to the experience of pleasure" (p. 5).

Previous research has found that savouring interventions can be effective at improving well-being of older adults. This pilot study examined the effects of a weeklong savouring intervention on older adults' psychological resilience and well-being (i.e., depressive symptoms and happiness). The participants, 111 adults aged 60 or over, completed measures of resilience, depression and happiness pre- and post-intervention as well as one month and three months after the intervention. Analyses revealed that participants who completed the savouring intervention also reported improvements in resilience and happiness as well as a reduction in depressive symptomatology over time (Smith & Hanni, 2017).

Where to from here?

Let's take a moment to reflect on what worked well. If you have your journal handy, give yourself five minutes to brainstorm about your experiences during *The Positivity Prescription*. Which *Positivity Practices* were the most powerful? Do you want to continue with them or give the ones that didn't work well another opportunity?

You might like to draw a line down the middle of your journal and create two columns, one for the *Positivity Practices* that worked well and one for those that didn't work so well.

Your wellbeing journey and commitment to becoming your best possible self has only just begun. To ensure your continued success, I recommend three additional *Positivity Practices*.

Creating Meaningful Goals

The use of goals is a powerful way to not only achieve our goals but to maintain successful changes, behaviours and rituals we've implemented. Having now completed *The Positivity Prescription,* I'm going to recommend that you engage in some structured goal setting to ensure sustained success.

Now is the time to explore any ANTS you have around goal setting, as they will definitely be blockers to your success. Given you've invested so much time and energy into completing the program, it would be a shame to stop now. I've written the book with the intention that this is a kick-start — not an end game. I'm going to suggest you set a goal for the next three months, however, as you'll see, the aim then will be to set another goal for the following three months (which will take you to six months).

Whilst research varies on how long it takes for behavioural changes to stick, I would recommend using goal setting until the six-month mark at least. If you're confident you don't need to continue to set goals at that point and you truly have nailed *The Positivity Prescription*, then feel free to abandon the structure and move towards more general intentions for who you want to be and how you want to live.

For now, I would suggest you consider setting a personal goal relating to your wellbeing, becoming your best self or creating your best life over the next six months.

If you are the person who started the program with an aim to immunise yourself against depression, having had struggles with your mood before or potentially a family history, then I would recommend that your goal be to continue to implement the strategies and skills to improve your mood, shift your mindset and improve your motivation.

If you are the person who wasn't concerned about depression, but definitely wasn't feeling their best and perhaps felt lost or uncertain about what matters most in life or their life direction, then I would recommend that your goal be to continue to implement the strategies and skills to lift your mood and motivation, but in addition leverage your strengths to find more meaning.

If you are the person who was doing pretty well already in being or becoming their best selves and in living their best lives and was primarily doing the program to learn additional skills, then I would recommend your goal be to determine which skills and strategies will help you stretch yourself and help others. Once your cup is full, it is much easier to help others.

But what if you have set goals before and failed or you prefer resolutions or intentions? Most of us have done some form of goal setting in the past, whether it is a New Year's resolution or when we have been asked to set a goal at work. If you have undertaken goal setting in a more structured way before, you will probably be familiar with the SMART acronym (specific, measurable, achievable, realistic and time-bound), which was derived from 30 years of research on goals (Locke & Latham, 2002).

However, not all goals are created equal. Research tells us that people often set goals to please others, such as our partners, parents or even health professionals. Do you remember the difference between intrinsic and extrinsic motivation (explored in Week 2: Motivation)? Research has confirmed that goals need to be authentic to create meaning. That is, they need to be aligned to our core life values.

Now that you know what your values are, it is going to be much easier to set a SMART goal that sticks:

Specific. Ensure your goals are clear and specific. For example, a fuzzy goal would be to feel better, while a specific goal would be to increase your levels of wellbeing by implementing a regular mindfulness practice three times a week.

Measurable. Find a way to measure your progress, such as with a wall chart or app to track your mindfulness sessions.

Authentic. I have replaced "achievable" goals with "authentic" goals here. Authentic goals are attractive and achievable when they are aligned with our core values and life vision. This is what makes our goals meaningful and is the most important aspect of goal setting, so do not leave it out!

Realistic. What evidence do you have that you can achieve this goal? Give yourself a reality check prior to embarking on your journey. Perhaps beginning a mindfulness practice with three sessions a week might be more realistic than trying to adhere to a seven-day a week practice. Yes, goals need to stretch us, however they become demotivating if we do not make the progress we expect.

Time-bound. We all know that setting a deadline helps us put in the effort needed. Three months is a good period to see observable change and determine success. Revisit your fuzzy vision and set shorter-term goals that act as stepping stones towards that vision.

Success Story

Alex's goal is "By the 31st of December, to have developed a plan designed to increase my wellbeing from 6 to 8 on a scale of 10 (where 0 is languishing and 10 is flourishing)."

Alex uses the SMART acronym to define and work towards her goal.

Specific. Alex will write and implement a three-month plan to increase her levels of positivity and general wellbeing. Alex's plan will consist of the three key *Positivity Practices* of gratitude, mindfulness and forgiveness.

Measurable. Alex will use a scale from 0 to 10 to track progress. Alex currently rates her wellbeing as a 6/10 and the goal is to rate an 8/10 at the end of the three months.

Authentic. The goal fits in with Alex's values of health, vitality, accomplishment and peace.

Realistic. For Alex, focusing on three key *Positivity Practices* for three months will be easier than trying to implement all 20 *Positivity Practices* at once. Alex already uses a gratitude journal so the aim will be to adhere to the practice three times a week. Alex also has a mindfulness practice, so the aim will be to adhere to it three times a week on alternate days to the gratitude practice. Alex has never trialled a forgiveness intervention. Alex aims to keep it simple by engaging in a growth mindset and letting go of at least one grudge.

Time-bound. Alex will review the plan in three months on the 31st of December to determine whether she has reached her goal and whether she wants to continue to use the three *Positivity Practices* for the next three months. Alex will also determine when she will introduce new *Positivity Practices* into her weekly timetable.

Positivity Practice #18: Setting Meaningful Goals

Take some time now to set a SMART goal. While you are free to select your own goal, as suggested earlier, I would recommend you set a general goal for *The Positivity Prescription* program around improving your positivity and wellbeing. This goal can also help you trial *Positivity Practices* within a goal-setting context. Use your existing journal to do this or, alternatively, you might like to start a new goal-setting journal that is dedicated to your goal.

Make sure to use the SMART acronym to break your goal down. I would also suggest you rate your commitment to the goal and your level of confidence in completing it.

Rating of commitment:

1   2   3   4   5   6   7   8   9   10

Rating of confidence:

1   2   3   4   5   6   7   8   9   10

Overcoming Obstacles

Most of us realise that setting and striving towards our goals is not always smooth sailing and that there will be many obstacles and distractions along the way.

The best thing to do is be prepared for as many setbacks as possible. Some will be easy to identify, however, some will come out of left field and it may be difficult to prepare for them.

Besides a Letter from the Future, many people use visualisation as a strategy to imagine the life they desire or the behavioural change they desire. In fact, visualisation is used extensively in Clinical Psychology for the treatment of anxiety and phobias to overcome fear. It's also used in Sports Psychology and Executive Coaching for peak performance.

Take a moment to recall times in the past when you have used this technique, whether this was explicit (for example on instruction from a coach, mentor or teacher) or more implicitly when you were daydreaming about your desires. Have you experienced success through visualisation before?

Professor Gabrielle Oettingen, an academic and expert in how people think about the future, has developed a method to anticipate and troubleshoot potential obstacles based on visualisation. Professor Oettingen's research found that rather than viewing and visualising our dreams, desires and goals as a rose-coloured optimist, where everything goes perfectly, it is far better to consider the potential obstacles to success prior to heading down the yellow brick road.

Professor Oettingen's method is known as WOOP (wish, outcome, obstacle and plan) (Oettingen, 1996). Using the WOOP method can enhance our chances of success and sustaining powerful behavioural change.

The WOOP Method

Take a few minutes to reflect on both your Letter from the Future and your SMART goal. Focus on the positive future outcome of fulfilling your life's desires. Now try and identify and imagine the most critical personal obstacles that might stand in the way of your success.

Brainstorm all the possible obstacles or challenges you may face in implementing the changes you desire. Finally, spend some time creating "if-then" statements for three potential obstacles. For example, "If I wake up too late for my morning mindfulness meditation, I will schedule a 10-minute session before I go to sleep", or, "If I'm struggling with challenging my ANTS, I'll seek professional assistance". "If-then" planning helps you proactively form a plan to overcome or circumvent obstacles when they occur on the way to fulfilling your dreams.

Potential obstacle	Plan to overcome the obstacle
1. If …	Then …
2. If …	Then …
3. If …	Then …

Staying on Track

Despite having a plan for when obstacles occur, many of us will still have difficulties in staying on track through the goal-striving process. One of the most powerful ways to stay on track with your goal-striving is coaching. You may have experienced coaching through a sporting activity or through your workplace, where it is increasingly being used to support peak performance. The good news is that we know coaching can enhance your chances of achieving your goals. The reason I am so passionate about coaching is that I have conducted four randomised controlled trials on evidence-based coaching to show that it increases both goal striving and wellbeing.

It's a double whammy, which is exactly what we are after in this program. The last thing we want is achievement at the cost of wellbeing. You will need to decide now which coaching option you are going to take. The reason I am asking you to commit to one of these options is to ensure we are doing everything we can to set you up for success.

The three options are:

- **Engage a professional coach** (you can refer to the resources list at the end of the book).

- **Find a co-coach**, someone who may be doing the program with you and who can support you through it and hold you accountable to the *Positivity Practices* you commit to each week.

- **Self-coach.** This is not for the faint-hearted or those low on grit or self-regulation. In this scenario, you would schedule in monthly self-coaching sessions during the program to ensure you are doing everything you have committed to.

Positivity Practice #19: Get a Coach
Decide now on your course of action to support you post-program.

Remember, you've invested time into completing the program over the last six weeks. Remind yourself of your values and vision and the best possible self you want to be.

Have you ever used a professional coach? It may not be as expensive as you think. I find that most people don't hesitate to invest in their external beauty but query the same amount that they may spend on beauty or gym memberships when it comes to committing to their own personal growth and intentionally designing a life they love.

If you're not able to commit to a professional coach, consider a co-coach, peer coach or supportive friend. Ideally, they will have completed *The Positivity Prescription* too and you can hold each other accountable post-program. I would suggest you either meet face-to-face, virtually or simply set up an email coaching arrangement where you're touching base at least once a month. This touchpoint gives you the opportunity to be clear on the "what" and "why" of your shorter-term goals and simultaneously remind you of your values and longer-term fuzzy vision.

Finally, the last option and my least preferred is self-coaching. As mentioned earlier, unless you have self-regulation as one of your signature strengths, you're unlikely to stick to this. Not due to laziness or that you simply don't care enough, it's just that life gets in the way! We prioritise other people, other commitments and our own dreams and desires can so quickly be pushed aside. I also find this commonly occurring for those who have kindness as a signature strength, whereby they spend an inordinate amount of time caring for others that their dreams and wellbeing can suffer.

Once you've decided on your course of action, do something that moves you towards that now before you complete this book. That might mean sending us an email for a recommendation, writing down the name of someone who could be your co-coach or scheduling in your first self-coaching session into your calendar with a monthly repeat session for the next three months.

Prioritising Positivity

In Week 1: Mood, I introduced you to the concept of prioritising positivity and the associated research. If you recall, people who prioritise positivity experience greater levels of wellbeing. In this week's homework, you'll have the opportunity to identify and include in your timetable some of the key *Positivity Practices* you've found helpful during the program and are already using successfully to support your wellbeing.

Recent research on prioritising positivity has found that for younger people, prioritising positivity has a significant impact on reducing negative emotions, whereas for older people, prioritising positivity has a significant impact on increasing positive emotions (Littman-Ovadia & Russo-Netzer, 2018). This research highlights the importance of both reducing negative emotions and increasing positive emotions, which we also highlighted in Week 1: Mood.

Littman-Ovadia and Russo-Netzer's (2018) research identified seven main themes of activities and situations that can be used to prioritise positivity:

- **Interpersonal relationships** (such as being with your kids or spending time with your partner).

- **Accomplishments** (such as closing a successful deal at work or achieving a good grade on your studies).

- **Pleasure** (such as listening to your favourite music or snuggling in front of the TV).

- **Creative activities** (such as engaging in your hobbies and creating new things).

- **Contributions to society** (such as volunteering or giving to charity).

- **Virtues or overall life view** (such as living according to your values and being hopeful and optimistic about the future).

- **Faith** (such as praying or attending a place of worship).

In Littman-Ovadia and Russo-Netzer's (2018) study, almost half of the people identified interpersonal relationships as a powerful means for increasing positive emotions, so make sure to focus on those.

Positivity Practice #20: Creating a Positive Life Timetable

Our final *Positivity Practice* is one that will help you stay on track by ensuring your life timetable supports your goal striving and moves you towards your dreams and desires. I have used this *Positivity Practice* successfully with clients for many years.

A life timetable gives you an overview of your ideal week or month. You can create one in a spreadsheet or write one by hand. Across the top of the timetable, list the days of the week. Down the left-hand side, list the hours of the day, starting at the time you wake. A tip here is to make that an early start as research supports that being an early bird enhances your wellbeing and performance.

The first step is to complete and review your current life timetable to see whether you want to make any changes, including removing commitments and activities. In my professional work, time and time again, I've found people overscheduling and trying to fit too much into their days, weeks and lives. I know I'm also guilty of this!

The opportunity now is to create a Positive Life Timetable that supports your wellbeing and moves you towards both your shorter-term goals and longer-term fuzzy vision (i.e. your dreams and desires).

I usually suggest that you lock in your work and family responsibilities first. Of course, we need to keep a roof over our heads and food on the table. We also have others we're responsible for or committed to.

Then lock in at least three exercise sessions a week. There is significant research to show that exercise is one of the most powerful wellbeing strategies available to us. Exercise positively impacts both our physical and mental health and wellbeing.

Now, the opportunity exists for you to prioritise positivity. Lock in and ritualise some of the *Positivity Practices* that have been working well for you during the program. This may be writing in your gratitude journal every evening or engaging in a regular mindfulness practice. Ensure that there is at least one activity a day that you know will increase your positive emotional state and/or reduce your negative emotional state.

Whether you've decided on a professional coach, co-coach or self-coaching to help you stay on track with your goals, you'll also need to monitor how well your Positive Life Timetable is doing to support your goal striving.

Another great strategy is to review your goals by seasons. The start of every season is the perfect time to revisit your fuzzy vision, revisit your goals from last season and set new goals for the new season.

You can also revisit your Positive Life Timetable and determine what you are going to remove and what you're going to introduce. It may be that winter is the perfect time to revisit your core life values as you find yourself hibernating at home with more time for self-reflection. Summer might be the perfect time to put your strengths to action or spot strengths in others through activities like learning to dance or sail.

Relating to Family and Friends During This Time

Before we conclude, I wanted to mention the power of our social connections in either supporting or undermining our success. Whilst *The Positivity Prescription* heavily relies on you as an individual in putting the knowledge and information into practice, it's important to note that research has shown that social support and positive relationships are key to our wellbeing and overall success.

However, most of us know that friends and family can also be a hindrance or blockage in helping us create positive changes. Sometimes, this means we hold back from sharing our dreams, desires and goals.

That is probably a wise decision when it comes to those who might not have our best interests at heart. Sometimes, people undermine our efforts (consciously or unconsciously) because it means our relationship with them will change. If we change, this might mean they need to take a hard look at themselves and their own lives.

For those who are on our side though (our cheerleaders), they cannot assist us unless they know what we are doing and why. Let your family, friends and supportive peeps know that you have started *The Positivity Prescription* and will continue with this program. Be sure to share which *Positivity Practices* worked well for you as this might inspire your friends and family to try them too.

Who will you share your good news with? Make some quick notes in your journal.

Setbacks, Relapse and Curve Balls

Even if you are having a dream run right now, we all know setbacks happen and the next curve ball is just around the corner. It's also really important to bear in mind the research we learned in Week 2: Motivation on the stages of change. Remember, relapse is normal.

If we expect relapse to occur, we're more likely to be proactive in planning for it, just like we've done with the WOOP method above. Be sure to put your skills into practice and consider upping the ante when setbacks occur. It's often when the curve balls come that we experience relapse and stop the *Positivity Practices* that we need more than ever! For example, we stop exercising or meditating.

I would suggest you refer back to *The Positivity Prescription* if you see a curve ball coming, find yourself in one unexpectedly or fall off the wagon where old habits re-emerge and *Positivity Practices* fall to the wayside. When we're in the eye of the storm, we often find it difficult to survive, let alone thrive. But having put your *Positivity Practices* to good use prior, you will be more experienced and accomplished at using the strategies when curve balls come.

Remember, don't be too hard on yourself when you relapse. This might be the time to revisit Week 6: Mindset, as it's likely you'll be experiencing a number of ANTS. It's important to cultivate kindness and self-compassion and get back on track. Return to your values and vision. Rest and regroup.

There are thousands of success stories of people who failed more times than they succeeded. In fact, failure was just par for the course! Rather than viewing the experience as a failure, see it as feedback as to what works and what you need to do differently. This is the time when a coach other than yourself can be helpful in supporting you to pick yourself up, dust yourself down and start again.

After the curve ball, setback or relapse, you will need to identify which *Positivity Practices* you want to re-introduce or increase during the curve-ball experience. The setback may also help you realise that other *Positivity Practices* might be key to your success, even ones you thought might not work, such as developing a lesser strength such as humility.

Take a moment now to make notes in your journal on what you will need to do to ensure you stay positive, particularly when you experience setbacks or relapse.

Farewell

Well here we are, at the end of the program and simultaneously at the beginning of your journey! Congratulations on completing *The Positivity Prescription*. Thank you for your commitment and courage in creating a flourishing life.

If you'd like a certificate of completion, contact us at info@thepositivityinstitute.com.au and we'll give you a brief test of knowledge and be happy to provide you with the certificate.

I would also love you to become part of The Positivity Institute family and help us create a flourishing world by spreading the information and strategies contained in this book. If you'd like to receive our monthly e-news and our free *Positivity Practices* Diary Card you can register via our website (www.thepositivityinstitute.com.au). Do not hesitate to reach out at info@thepositivityinstitute.com.au if you need further help or would like to provide feedback on the program.

If you love the content of this book, and you think this information will be valuable in your workplace, please contact us for more information on our POTENTIAL+ corporate program.

You can also get just as much out of reading this book and practising the self-coaching exercises at home.

Until then, stay well and stay positive!

Dr Suzy Green ✤

The 7th M: Mental Toughness

"You don't have to be the loudest in the room, but you do have to be the toughest."

MICHELLE OBAMA

Welcome to our bonus chapter on the 7th M - Mental Toughness! Now strictly speaking Mental Toughness (MT) is not another discrete psychological capability like each of the 6Ms, but a model and framework that will help you prepare for and manage daily hassles or larger life stressors. So far this book has been focused primarily on the proactive promotion of mental health and wellbeing, which is relatively easy to do when things are going well in life, however much harder to do when they're not! So, in this chapter, I'll be helping you apply all you've learned so far about the six key psychological capabilities (the 6Ms) to support you when things are a little more challenging. You'll discover how increasing your Mental Toughness (MT) through application of the 6Ms can help you enhance your ability to navigate challenges, persist through adversity, and thrive under pressure.

In this chapter we'll be focusing on:

1. **The Science of Mental Toughness** – Understanding what it is and why it matters.

2. **Assessing Your Mental Toughness** – Identifying where you currently stand using the 4C Model.

3. **Strengthening Your Mental Toughness** – Leveraging practical strategies for Control, Commitment, Confidence, and Challenge.

4. **Applying the 6Ms to help build your Mental Toughness** – Applying key psychological capabilities to build resilience and fortitude.

The Science of Mental Toughness

Mental Toughness is a psychological trait that enables individuals to **perform under pressure, stay resilient in adversity, and maintain emotional stability.** Research highlights that those with higher MT experience greater **wellbeing, motivation, and success** across various aspects of life.

Mental Toughness is defined as:

"A personality trait which significantly determines how individuals perform when exposed to stressors, pressure and challenge.... irrespective of the prevailing situation."

Clough & Strycharczyk, 2011

The 4C Model of Mental Toughness

Developed by Clough and Strycharczyk (2011), the **4C Model of Mental Toughness** identifies four core dimensions that contribute to an individual's ability to thrive under pressure. These dimensions are **Control, Commitment, Confidence, and Challenge.**

- **Control** refers to the extent to which individuals believe they have influence over their environment and emotions. Those with high control maintain composure in stressful situations and believe they can shape their own outcomes.

- **Commitment** reflects the ability to set and stay dedicated to goals, demonstrating perseverance despite obstacles. High commitment individuals are reliable, disciplined, and focused on achieving their objectives.

- **Confidence** encompasses both self-belief in abilities and interpersonal confidence—allowing individuals to trust in their competence and assert themselves effectively in social and professional settings.

- **Challenge** relates to how individuals perceive difficulties as opportunities for growth rather than threats. Those who score high in challenge embrace change and view setbacks as learning experiences.

From the image below, you'll note that each of the 4Cs has two sub-components (or scales, as they're referred to in the scientific literature). For example, confidence includes both "confidence in abilities" and "interpersonal confidence." In my experience, someone can be high in "confidence in abilities" but have lower levels of "interpersonal confidence"!

The 4C model has been widely applied in sports, business, and education, demonstrating that individuals with higher levels of MT perform better, manage stress effectively, and maintain motivation in the face of setbacks. Understanding and developing these four dimensions is key to building resilience and sustaining high performance in various aspects of life.

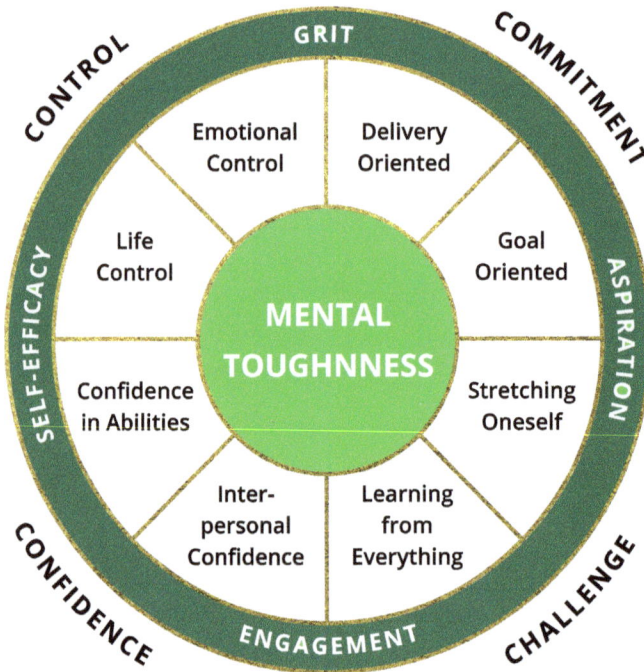

Why is Mental Toughness Important?

Performance:
- Better use of psychological strategies to improve performance (Crust & Azadi, 2010, Mattie & Munroe-Chandler, 2012).
- Better able to redirect attention (Dewhurst et al., 2012).
- Associated with age and managerial seniority (Marchant et al., 2009).

Behaviour:
- Acquisition and retention of skills (Moradi et al., 2013).
- More likely to perceive a situation as a challenge (vs. threat) (Levy et al., 2012).

- More likely to take risks (Crust & Keegan, 2010).
- More likely to persist with a challenge (Nussbaum & Dweck, 2008).
- Better disciplined e.g., attendance (St Clair-Thompson et al., 2014).

Wellbeing:
- Deal better with stress and pressure (Gerber et al., 2012a).
- Sleep better (Brand et al., 2011).
- Have better relationships (St Clair-Thompson et al., 2014).
- Less likely to develop mental health issues (Gerber et al., 2013).
- Better able to manage their own emotions (Crust, 2009).
- More likely to exercise (Gerber et al., 2013).

Aspiration:
- Perform better academically (St Clair-Thompson, 2014).
- Better classroom behaviour (St Clair-Thompson, 2014).
- Show higher resilience (Gerber et al., 2012a).
- Show more optimism and coping skills (Nicholls et al., 2008).

Measuring Mental Toughness

A key aspect of developing Mental Toughness is accurately assessing where you currently stand. The **Mental Toughness Questionnaire** (MTQ+)* is a scientifically validated tool designed to measure Mental Toughness across the **4C Model**—Control, Commitment, Confidence, and Challenge. The MTQ+ consists of a series of questions that evaluate an individual's ability to manage stress, remain committed to goals, maintain confidence in their abilities, and embrace challenges as opportunities for growth. *If you'd like to take the*

MTQ+, contact us at The Positivity Institute.

Why Use the MTQ+?

The MTQ+:

• Provides a **detailed breakdown** of Mental Toughness levels across the 4Cs.

• Helps identify **strengths and areas for improvement** in resilience and performance.

• Is used widely in **sports, education, leadership, and workplace settings** to enhance performance and wellbeing.

• Offers insights that can inform **personal development plans and coaching strategies.**

By understanding your Mental Toughness profile through the w+, you can take targeted actions to enhance your ability to navigate challenges effectively.

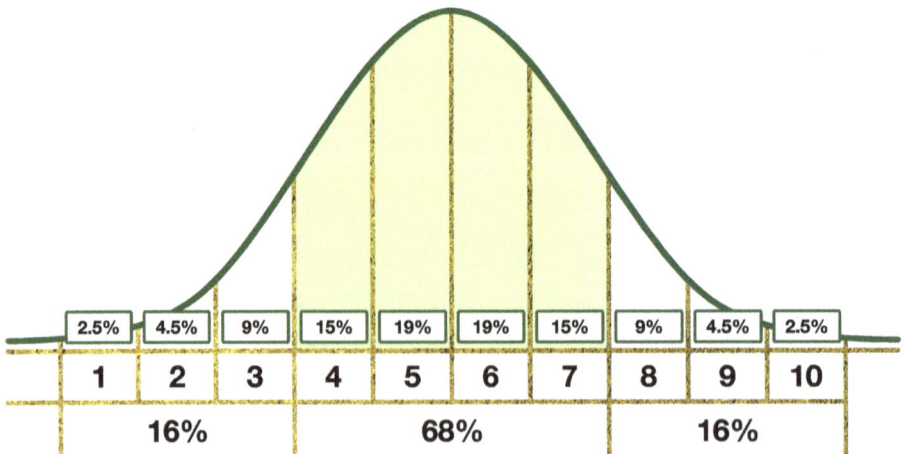

2.5%	4.5%	9%	15%	19%	19%	15%	9%	4.5%	2.5%
1	2	3	4	5	6	7	8	9	10

16%   68%   16%

Assessing Your Mental Toughness: Where Are You Now?

Using the **4C Model**, you can determine your strengths and areas for improvement in MT:

- **Control:** Do you believe you can shape your outcomes and regulate emotions effectively?

- **Commitment:** Are you able to set and stick to long-term goals?

- **Confidence:** How strongly do you believe in your own abilities and interpersonal effectiveness?

- **Challenge:** Do you view obstacles as opportunities for growth rather than threats?

Before you self-assess along these four dimensions, read the descriptions below of what high and low levels of MT look like. Also note that when it comes to descriptions of lower levels of MT, the preferred term is "mental sensitivity", not mental weakness! For a little self-disclosure, I truly believe I would have rated much lower on MT earlier on in my life, with a family history of anxiety and depression, and it's only through my psychological training and now maturity and life experience, that I can say I have developed high levels of MT!

High Mental Toughness

Those with high mental toughness:

- Have the capability to withstand a significant amount of pressure.

- Have confidence in their abilities and are often willing to take on demanding tasks, believing they will succeed.

- Can usually shrug off criticism and not take others' comments to heart.

- Are likely to speak their mind when working in groups and are usually comfortable in many different social and work contexts.

- Are committed to the task at hand, tenacious and resolute, and likely to complete what they start.

- When problems arise, they are unlikely to give up and typically view such events as challenges and opportunities for personal development rather than threats to their security.

- Tend to be in control of their emotions and can cope with difficult events, usually remaining calm and stable under pressure.

Low Mental Toughness

Those with low mental toughness:

- May find it difficult to cope with stressful and highly demanding environments.

- May suffer from a lack of self-belief.

- May find it hard to deal with criticism and will probably take others' comments too much to heart—also self-critical.

- May not be willing to push themselves forward enough, possibly because of a belief that they will not succeed.

- May avoid challenging situations for fear of failure and hence may not take all their opportunities for personal development.

- May worry about things unduly, sometimes getting problems out of perspective.

Self-Assessment Exercise

Rate yourself on a scale of **1 (low) to 10 (high)** for each of the 4Cs below. Note that each of the 4Cs has two components. Identify one area to focus on improving this week.

Commitment

"Courage and perseverance have a magical talisman, before which difficulties disappear and obstacles vanish into air."

John Quincy Adams

Commitment is a measure of how and why we set goals and how we respond to them (Clough & Strycharczyk, 2012). Individuals differ in the degree to which they remain focused on their goals. Some are easily distracted, bored or divert attention to other goals.

A high scorer on commitment will be able to *"see it through"* when faced with tough and unyielding deadlines and competing tasks. A low scorer will require a greater level of support to manage the demands of stress at work.

Research on mental toughness has identified two subscales for this component:

Achievement oriented: individuals high on this subscale will work hard on goals and are conscientious, focused and concentrated.

Your Score/Self-Scoring

1	2	3	4	5	6	7	8	9	10
Low									High

Goal oriented: Individuals high on this subscale like working towards goals and targets, are motivated by them, and are easily able to visualise success.

Your Score/Self-Scoring

1	2	3	4	5	6	7	8	9	10
Low									High

Challenge

"Accept challenges, so that you may feel the exhilaration of victory."

George S. Patton

This component of MT addresses how we respond to challenges. A challenge represents any activity or event we see as out of the ordinary and involves doing something that stretches people outside their comfort zone.

Individuals differ in their approach to challenges. Those who score high on this scale thrive in continually changing environments. At the other end, we find those who prefer to minimise exposure to change and the problems that often come with it.

Research on MT has identified two subscales for this component:

Risk orientation: Individuals high on this subscale will stretch themselves to try new things and seek out challenging opportunities.

Your Score/Self-Scoring

1	2	3	4	5	6	7	8	9	10
Low									High

Learning orientation: Individuals high on this subscale enjoy learning new things and see setbacks as opportunities to learn.

Your Score/Self-Scoring

1	2	3	4	5	6	7	8	9	10
Low									High

Confidence

"It's not who we are that holds us back, it's who we think we're not."

Michael Nolan

Confidence measures the extent to which we have self-belief in our ability to see through to the conclusion of a difficult task that can be beset with setbacks.

Those with high levels of confidence will accept setbacks as part and parcel of everyday life. When these occur, confident people will take them in their stride. Those with overall low levels of confidence will see the same setback in a different way. They are more likely to feel defeated and accept that what has happened is so significant that it will prevent them from achieving the goal or task. They are more likely to give up.

Research on MT has identified two subscales for this component:

Confidence (Abilities): Individuals scoring high on this scale are more likely to believe they are a truly worthwhile person. They are less dependent on external validation and tend to be more optimistic about life in general.

Your Score/Self-Scoring

1	2	3	4	5	6	7	8	9	10
Low									High

Confidence (Interpersonal): Individuals scoring high on this scale tend to be more assertive. They are less likely to be intimidated in social settings and are more likely to promote themselves in groups. They are also better able to handle difficult or awkward people.

Your Score/Self-Scoring

1	2	3	4	5	6	7	8	9	10
Low									High

Control

"Destiny is as destiny does. If you believe you have no control, then you have no control."

Wess Roberts

The more we believe we can shape and influence what is happening around us, the more likely we are to feel we can make a difference and achieve what is necessary. Studies consistently show that the less people feel they are in control, the more likely they are to feel more stressed, which leads to negative consequences. The control dimension of MT is closely related to learned helplessness and pessimism.

Research on MT has shown there are two components – life control and emotional control.

Emotional Control: Individuals scoring high on this scale are better able to manage their emotions. They can keep anxieties in check and are less likely to reveal their emotional state to other people. Scores on emotional control correlate negatively with neuroticism, i.e. individuals with greater emotional control have lower levels of neuroticism (worry and anxiety).

Your Score/Self-Scoring

1	2	3	4	5	6	7	8	9	10
Low									High

Life Control: Individuals scoring high on this are more likely to believe they are "masters" of their destiny. They feel that their plans will not be thwarted and that they can make a difference.

Your Score/Self-Scoring

1	2	3	4	5	6	7	8	9	10
Low									High

Developing Mental Toughness

Can MT be developed? Sports psychologists and coaches would argue they have been doing this for years! Growing evidence shows that mental skills training can lead to self-reported increases in mental toughness (Gucciardi et al., 2009a).

Below are some strategies of how you can apply the 6Ms in situations of stress, pressure and challenge to build MT. You might like to identify one specific situation at work/life where you need to develop your MT. Use that to reflect on the strategies discussed.

One recommendation I'd make is to first asterisk or highlight the strategies below that you're doing well already and could up the ante when adversity strikes. Then also identify strategies you're less familiar with and refer to the relevant chapter to learn more! Perhaps re-read the Motivation chapter (week 2) to remind you why you're persisting with this program for both the proactive enhancement of your mental health and wellbeing and the prevention of mental ill health.

One way to think about this is through the circles of concern, influence and control. As the image below shows, while there are many things that are outside of our control or influence, one thing we can control – well, maybe not easily – but can learn to manage better – is our thoughts and behaviours! Hence, the 6Ms come in!

Circles of Concern, Influence and Control

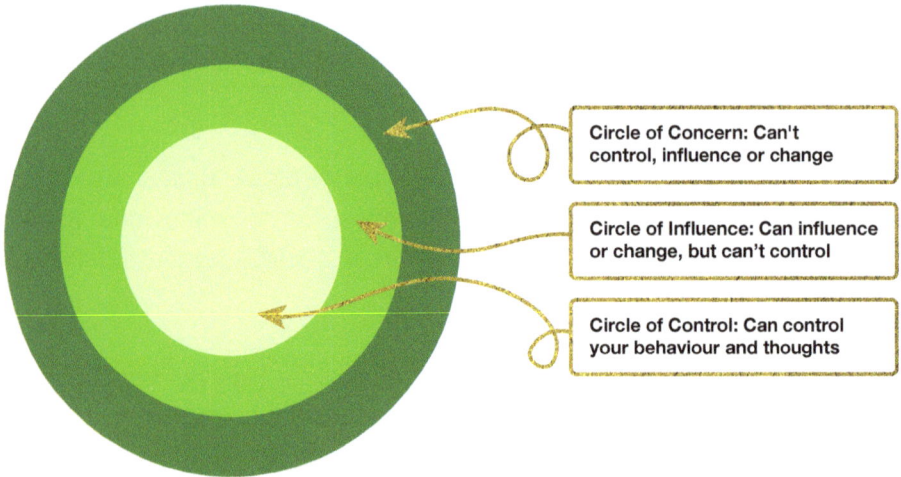

Circle of Concern: Can't control, influence or change

Circle of Influence: Can influence or change, but can't control

Circle of Control: Can control your behaviour and thoughts

It is more effective to spend time and energy on what you can control. The challenge is to stretch yourself to widen your circle of control.

Applying the 6Ms to Build Mental Toughness

The 6M Model provides a structured approach to building MT by applying six key psychological capabilities. Each of the 6Ms—**Mindset, Mood, Mindfulness, Might, Meaning, and Motivation**—plays a crucial role in developing resilience and the ability to persist through adversity.

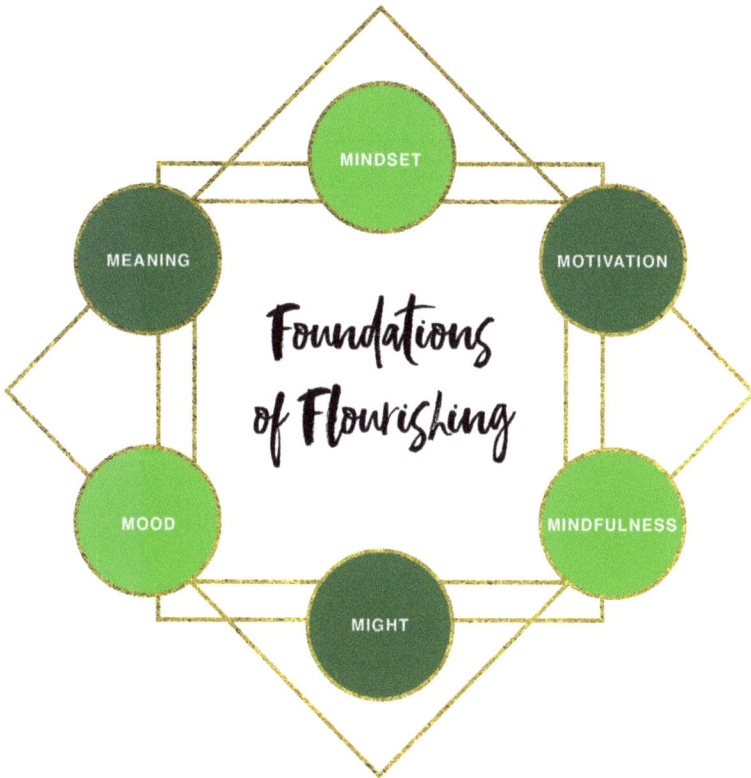

Mood: Harnessing Positive Emotions for Strength

Research shows positive emotions are crucial in broadening our thinking and building psychological resources. Engaging in practices like gratitude, acts of kindness, and savouring experiences enhances emotional stability and strengthens resilience in difficult times. One particularly effective strategy is prioritising positivity—intentionally making space for activities that generate positive emotions, even when stress levels are high. When faced with adversity, we often neglect the very habits that sustain us, such as exercise or social connection. However, research on the Broaden-and-Build Theory (covered in Week 1: Mood) highlights that cultivating emotions like gratitude, hope, and love counteracts the narrowing effects of stress and fear, fostering cognitive flexibility, creative problem-solving, and emotional regulation. Additionally, the undoing effect of positive emotions helps the body recover from stress by down-regulating negative emotional and physiological states, restoring balance, and enabling us to approach challenges with greater adaptability. By consciously amplifying positivity, we enhance our capacity to navigate adversity with strength and resourcefulness.

Mood boosting strategies to apply:

Engage in **gratitude exercises** to shift focus towards positivity.

- Use **savouring techniques** to reinforce positive experiences.

- Leverage **acts of kindness** to build emotional resilience.

- **Let go of grudges** to release anger and positively impact your energy levels!

- Up the ante on **prioritising positivity** to broaden and build your thoughts, emotions and behaviours.

Motivation: Maintaining Drive and Momentum

When the going gets tough, it's crucial to realign with our values, vision, and goals. As we explored in Motivation in week 2, setting clear, value-driven goals fosters a sense of progress and determination, helping us stay focused even in the face of adversity. High levels of intrinsic motivation—truly understanding your why—play a vital role in sustaining long-term perseverance and success. This becomes especially important when navigating prolonged, challenging situations, where resilience and a deep connection to purpose can make all the difference in pushing forward.

Motivational strategies to apply:

Set **long-term goals with actionable steps.**

- Create **short-term daily strategies** to overcome procrastination. For example, set a 15-minute timer for a break and then return to the task at hand.

- **Develop intrinsic motivation through revisiting your core life values** to remind yourself of your "why" for pursuing your goals.

Might: Utilising Strengths to Build Resilience

Leveraging personal strengths is a powerful way to build self-efficacy and confidence, particularly in the face of adversity. Identifying and applying strengths in new and creative ways enhances perseverance and reinforces a sense of agency during challenging times. Research consistently shows that a strengths-based approach contributes to greater wellbeing, and adopting this perspective during adversity—or in proactively preparing for future challenges—can be especially transformative. It not only allows you to harness and flex your signature strengths but also provides an opportunity to develop your lesser strengths (bottom five), which may be particularly valuable if bravery happens to be one of them! By intentionally cultivating both well-developed and emerging strengths, you expand your capacity for resilience and growth.

Might strategies to apply:

Identify and apply **signature strengths** in daily life.

- Engage in **strength-spotting** to recognise resilience in others.

- Apply **strengths-based goal-setting** to align strengths with long-term aspirations.

- Review the description of your **Best Possible Self** and visualise yourself successfully leveraging your strengths to overcome the challenges you're facing.

Meaning: Aligning with Purpose and Values

When adversity strikes, especially when facing a prolonged and challenging journey, a strong sense of meaning becomes essential. There will be moments when everything feels overwhelming and giving up seems like the easier option. During those times, reconnecting with your personal values and purpose can provide the intrinsic motivation needed to stay committed to your goals.

Techniques like the Letter from the Future or the Best Possible Self exercise can serve as powerful reminders of your long-term aspirations, reinforcing a sense of meaning and resilience for the road ahead.

Meaning strategies to apply:

- Reflect on **your core values** and how you can use them to face your challenge.

- Engage in **Best Possible Self visualisation** to clarify aspirations.

- Review your **personal purpose statement** to reinforce motivation.

- **Identify small actions** you can take to move forward, in a values-congruent way, despite feelings of uncertainty and anxiety.

Mindfulness: Enhancing Self-Regulation and Awareness

During stressful times, mindfulness is essential for maintaining emotional balance and resilience. Cultivating present-moment awareness helps individuals recognise Automatic Negative Thoughts (ANTs) (refer to Mindset Week 6 chapter) before they spiral into heightened stress or anxiety. Instead of reacting impulsively, mindfulness allows us to pause—creating space to observe these thoughts with curiosity rather than judgment. This awareness enables the application of evidence-based strategies like the ABCDE method (see Mindset Week 6 chapter), helping to reframe unhelpful thinking patterns and foster a more constructive mindset. Strengthening attentional control and self-awareness through mindfulness techniques, such as those listed in Mindfulness Week 5, enables individuals to regulate their emotions and remain composed under pressure.

Mindfulness strategies to apply:

- Develop a daily **mindfulness meditation practice.**

- During stress, use the **STOP technique** (Stop, Take a breath, Observe, Proceed).

- Maintain a **mindfulness journal** to track emotional responses.

Mindset: Cultivating a Growth-Oriented Mentality

Mindset plays a powerful role in how we navigate adversity and cultivate resilience. Recognising and shifting away from a fixed mindset, where challenges are seen as insurmountable obstacles, is key to fostering adaptability and perseverance. By cultivating a growth mindset, we can view difficulties as opportunities for learning and development, enhancing our ability to thrive under pressure. Additionally, practicing Learned Optimism helps reframe setbacks by shifting our explanatory style—seeing adversity as temporary and changeable rather than permanent and personal. By disputing negative thoughts and consciously adopting a more constructive perspective, we strengthen our psychological resilience, empowering ourselves to approach challenges confidently and with a sense of possibility.

Mindset strategies to apply:

- Recognise and challenge **Automatic Negative Thoughts (ANTs).**

- Apply the **ABCDE Model** to reframe setbacks and failures.

- Engage in **self-reflection journaling** to identify patterns in thought distortions.

- Build **psychological flexibility** through Acceptance and Commitment Therapy (ACT) techniques.

Conclusion

Mental Toughness is a critical skill that enhances resilience, performance, and overall wellbeing. It is not about being immune to stress but about **managing it effectively, persisting through adversity, and cultivating confidence when facing challenges.** By implementing the strategies outlined in this chapter and regularly practicing the Challenge Checklist below, individuals can build a strong foundation for MT and flourish in all aspects of life. Developing MT is an ongoing journey that leads to a more resilient, determined, and empowered version of yourself. ❉

Challenge Checklist

To reinforce Mental Toughness, complete the following:

☐ **Assess Yourself:** Complete the MTQ+ assessment and reflect on your results. Where are your strengths? What opportunities do you have for MT development?

☐ **Track Your Mindset:** Catch your negative thought patterns (ANTS) and replace them with performance enhancing affirmations (PETS).

☐ **Build Emotional Control:** Practice mindfulness and breathing exercises during stressful moments.

☐ **Commit to a Challenge Goal:** Set a SMART goal that pushes you out of your comfort zone and track your progress.

☐ **Confidence Challenge:** Identify a role model who embodies resilience, reinforcing your belief that growth and achievement are possible through effort and perseverance

ABOUT THE AUTHOR

Dr Suzy Green, D.Psyc.(Clin.) MAPS
Founder & CEO, The Positivity Institute

Dr Suzy Green is a Clinical and Coaching Psychologist (MAPS) and Founder & CEO of The Positivity Institute, a Sydney-based positively deviant organisation dedicated to the research and application of the science of optimal human functioning in organisations and schools.

Suzy is a leader in the complementary fields of Coaching Psychology and Positive Psychology having conducted a world-first study on evidence-based coaching as an Applied Positive Psychology. She has published over twenty academic chapters and peer reviewed journal articles including the Journal of Positive Psychology. She is also the co-editor of "Positive Psychology Coaching in Practice" (Green & Palmer, 2018), "Positive Psychology Coaching in the Workplace" (Smith, Boniwell & Green, 2021) and "The Positivity Prescription" (Green, 2019).

Suzy lectured on Applied Positive Psychology as a Senior Adjunct Lecturer in the Coaching Psychology Unit, University of Sydney for ten years and is an Honorary Vice President of the International Society for Coaching Psychology. Suzy is an Honorary Professor at the UTS Business School, Sydney, and a Visiting Professor at the University of East London, and an Honorary Fellow at the University of Melbourne. Suzy is also a member of the Scientific Advisory Board for CoachHub, a leading global coaching technology platform.

Suzy retains a small number of senior executive/c-suite coaching clients supporting their performance and wellbeing. Suzy's expertise is in developmental/transformational coaching. This type of coaching takes a broader strategic approach, often dealing with issues relating to personal and professional growth. This enables the client to create a fundamental shift in their capacity to change their thinking, feeling and behaviour. Coaching sessions may focus on facilitating insight, enhancing emotional competencies, or creating and sustaining positive relationships. The coaching sessions provide a reflective space where the client can explore issues and options and formulate action plans. ❊

Instagram: @drsuzy and @the.positivity.institute · Facebook: The Positivity Institute

ACKNOWLEDGEMENTS

Given this book has been 20 years in the making, there are many people I want to thank in bringing this book to life.

Firstly, Professor Lindsay Oades and the late Professor Anthony Grant, my doctoral supervisors (2001–2003), without whose support, courage and commitment I wouldn't bewhere I am today and this book would not exist. They saw strengths in me that I couldn't see for myself at the time. I'm particularly thankful for their visionary leadership in a field where cynicism resided in the early days, particularly in academic settings. Their support and encouragement led me to a path of truly living my calling, despite much anxiety, as I put my strengths to use in the fields of Positive Psychology and Coaching Psychology. Amazingly, these research fields have grown substantially over the past 25 years and I consider myself fortunate and proud to have been there from the very beginning here in Australia.

Much gratitude also goes to my late and much loved parents, Valma and Maurice, who gaveme every opportunity to be the best I can be. My partner too, Glenn, whose unwavering belief in me and super self-regulatory coaching style helped me commit to goals and timelines in order to achieve my dream. His patience in sharing our precious time as a couple when I completed the book over many "writing weekends" is also greatly appreciated.

I am also grateful to my team at The Positivity Institute, Tracy, Jane, Claudia and Jaye who have also encouraged me to be gritty with my goal despite multiple distractions and who very much "walk the talk" of positivity at The Positivity Institute HQ. Thanks also to my many colleagues who so generously shared their knowledge and energy with me every day as we bring the science of optimal human functioning to life! ✤

RESOURCES

WEEK 1: MOOD

Recommended Books

- Bryant, F. B., & Veroff, J. (2007). Savoring: A new model of positive experience. Lawrence Erlbaum Associates Publishers.
- Emmons, R. (2007). *Thanks: How the new science of gratitude can make you happy.* New York, NY: Houghton Mifflin.
- Fredrickson, B. (2009). *Positivity.* New York, NY: Random House.
- Fredrickson, B. (2013). *Love 2.0.* New York, NY: Penguin Putnam Inc.
- Haidt, J. (2006). *The Happiness Hypothesis.* New York, NY: Basic Books.
- Kashdan, T., & Biswas-Diener, R. (2015). *The Upside of Your Dark Side.* New York, NY: Plume Books.
- Lyubomirsky, S. (2007). *The How of Happiness.* New York, NY: Penguin Putnam Inc.

Recommended Websites

- PEP Lab: www.peplab.web.unc.edu/
- Sonja Lyubomirsky: www.sonjalyubomirsky.com/
- The How of Happiness: www.thehowofhappiness.com/
- Scott Barry Kaufman: www.scottbarrykaufman.com/
- The Gottman Institute: www.gottman.com/
- The Black Dog Institute depression self-test: www.blackdoginstitute.org.au/resources-support/digital-tools-apps/depression-self-test/
- Everett Worthington's REACH forgiveness model: www.evworthington-forgiveness.com/reach-forgiveness-of-others

WEEK 2: MOTIVATION

Recommended Books

- Prochaska, O. J., Norcross, C. J., & DiClemente, C. C. (1995). *Changing for Good.* New York, NY: Harper Collins.

- Grant, T & Greene, J. (2003). *Coach Yourself*. London, England: Pearson Education Limited.
- Deci, L. E., & Ryan, M. R. (2004) *Handbook of Self-Determination Research*. New York, NY: University of Rochester Press.
- George, B., & Sims, P. (2007). *True North: Discover Your Authentic Leadership*. San Francisco, CA: Jossey-Bass & John Wiley & Sons.
- Barrett, R. (2018). *Everything I Have Learned About Values*. Morrisville, NC: Lulu Publishing Services.
- Oettingen, G. (2014). *Rethinking Positive Thinking: Inside the New Science of Motivation*. New York, NY: Penguin Random House.
- Johnson, S. (2007). *The Present*. London, England: Transworld Publishers Ltd.

Recommended Websites

- B. J. Fogg's Tiny Habits: www.bjfogg.com/learn
- Self-determination theory: www.selfdeterminationtheory.org
- Transtheoretical model of the Cancer Prevention Research Center: www.web.uri.edu/cprc/transtheoretical-model/
- Barrett Values Centre: www.valuescentre.com

WEEK 3: MIGHT

Recommended Books

- Rath, T. (2015). *Strengths Finder 2.0*. Omaha, NE: Gallup Press.
- Buckingham, M., & Clifton, D.O. (2005). *Now, Discover Your Strengths*. New York, NY: Simon & Schuster.
- Yeager, J., Fisher, S. & Shearon, D. (2011). *Smart Strengths: Building Character, Resilience and Relationships in Youth*. New York, NY: Kravis Publishing.
- Polly, S., & Britton, K. H. (2015). *Character Strengths Matter*. San Francisco, CA: Positive Psychology News.
- Niemiec, R.M. & Wedding, D. (2008). *Positive Psychology at the Movies*. Toronto, Canada: Hogrefe & Huber.

Recommended Websites

- Free VIA strengths survey: www.viacharacter.org
- Various strengths assessments and reports: www.gallupstrengthscenter.com
- Michelle McQuaid: www.michellemcquaid.com/

WEEK 4: MEANING

Recommended Books

- Damon, W. (2008). *The Path to Purpose: How Young People Find Their Calling in Life.* New York, NY: The Free Press.
- Deki, J. B., Byrne, S. Z., & Steger, F. M. (2013). *Purpose and Meaning in the Workplace.* Washington, D.C.: American Psychological Society.
- Frankl, V. (2008). *Man's Search for Meaning.* London, England: Random House.
- Wong, P. T. P. (Ed.). (2012). *The Human Quest for Meaning.* (2nd Ed). New York, NY: Routledge Publishers.

Recommended Websites

- Paul Wong: www.drpaulwong.com
- Michael Steger: www.michaelfsteger.com

WEEK 5: MINDFULNESS

Recommended Books

- Bunting, M. (2016). Mindful Leadership. *7 Practices for Transforming Your Leadership, Your Organisation and Your Life.* Milton, Aus: Wiley.
- Carroll, M. (2008). The Mindful Leader. Boston, MA: Shambhala Publications.
- Goleman, D. (2014). Focus: The Hidden Driver of Excellence. London, England: Bloomsbury Publishing PLC.
- Kabat-Zinn, J. (1994). *Wherever You Go, There You Are: Mindfulness Meditation in Everyday Life.* New York, NY: Hyperion.
  McKenzie, S., & Hassed, C. (2012). *Mindfulness for Life.* Wollombi, NSW: Exisle Publishing.

- Niemiec, R. M. (2013). *Mindfulness and Character Strengths: A Practical Guide to Flourishing.* Toronto, ON: Hogrefe Publishing.
- Puddicombe, A. (2012). *The Headspace Guide to Meditation & Mindfulness.* London, England: Hodder & Stoughton General Division.
- Ricard, M. (2015). *Happiness: A Guide to Developing Life's Most Important Skill.* London, England: Atlantic Books.
- Tolle, E. (2001). *The Power of Now: A Guide to Spiritual Enlightenment.* London, England: Hodder & Stoughton.

Recommended Mindfulness Apps

- Smiling Mind
- 1GiantMind
- Headspace
- Insight Timer

Recommended Courses

- Meditation & Mindfulness Teacher Training, School of Positive Transformation: www.schoolofpositivetransformation.com/meditation-and-mindfulness-teacher-training/

Recommended Websites

- Smiling Mind: www.smilingmind.com.au
- Headspace: www.headspace.com
- 1 Giant Mind: www.1giantmind.com
- Potential Project: www.potentialproject.com

WEEK 6: MINDSET

Recommended Books

- Edelman, S. (2007). *Change Your Thinking.* New York, NY: Marlowe.
- Harris, R. (2008). *The Happiness Trap: How to Stop Struggling and Start Living.* Boston, MA: Trumpeter.
- Kahneman, D. (2004). *Thinking Fast and Slow.* New York, NY: Farrar, Straus and Giroux.

- Dweck, C. S. (2006). *Mindset: The New Psychology of Success.* New York, NY: Random House.
- Hayes, S. (2005). *Get out of Your Mind and into Your Life.* Oakland, CA: New Harbinger Publications.
- Banaji, M., & Greenwald, A. (2013). *Blindspot.* New York, NY: Bantam Books.
- Kornfield, J. (2002). *A Path with Heart.* London, England: Ebury Publishing.

Recommended Websites

- Beck Institute for Cognitive Behaviour Therapy: www.beckinstitute.org
- Mindset Works: www.mindsetworks.com/science
- Carol Dweck's Mindset: www.mindsetonline.com
- Authentic Happiness: www.authentichappiness.sas.upenn.edu/

Mental Health Services And Hotlines

Australia

- Lifeline: www.lifeline.org.au/
- Beyond Blue: www.beyondblue.org.au/get-support/national-help-lines-and-websites
- MensLine Australia: mensline.org.au/
- Mental Health First Aid: www.mentalhealthfirstaid.org
- RUOK: www.ruok.org.au/
- BlackDog Institute: www.blackdoginstitute.org.au/getting-help/

REFERENCES

Aknin, L. B., Dunn, E. W., & Norton, M. I. (2012). Happiness runs in a circular motion: Evidence for a positive feedback loop between prosocial spending and happiness. *Journal of Happiness Studies,* 13(2), 347-355.

Barrett, B., Hayney, M. S., Muller, D., Rakel, D., Ward, A., Obasi, C. N., ... West, R. (2012). Meditation or exercise for preventing acute respiratory infection: a randomized controlled trial. *The Annals of Family Medicine,* 10(4), 337-346.

Baumeister, R. F., Bratslavsky, E., Muraven, M., & Tice, D. M. (1998). Ego depletion: Is the active self a limited resource? *Journal of Personality and Social Psychology,* 74(5), 1252.

Baumeister, R. F., & Vohs, K. D. (2002). The pursuit of meaningfulness in life. In C. R. Snyder & S. J. Lopez (Eds.), *Handbook of positive psychology* (pp. 608-618). New York, NY: Oxford University Press.

Beck, A. T. (1967). *Depression: Clinical, experimental, and theoretical aspects.* New York, NY: University of Pennsylvania Press.

Berg, J. M., Grant, A. M., & Johnson, V. (2010). When callings are calling: Crafting work and leisure in pursuit of unanswered occupational callings. *Organization Science,* 21(5), 973-994.

Berg, J. M., Wrzesniewski, A., & Dutton, J. E. (2010). Perceiving and responding to challenges in job crafting at different ranks: When proactivity requires adaptivity. *Journal of Organizational Behavior,* 31(2-3), 158-186.

Buchanan, A., & Kern, M. L. (2017). The benefit mindset: The psychology of contribution and everyday leadership. *International Journal of Wellbeing,* 7(1), 1-11.

Buchanan, G. M., & Seligman, M. E. P. (Eds.). (1995). Explanatory style. Hillsdale, NJ: Lawrence Erlbaum Associates, Inc.

Buckingham, M., & Clifton, D. O. (2001). *Now, discover your strengths.* New York, NY: Simon and Schuster.

Brown, K. W., & Ryan, R. M. (2003). The benefits of being present: mindfulness and its role in psychological well-being. *Journal of Personality and Social Psychology,* 84(4), 822-848.

Brown, K. W., Ryan, R. M., & Creswell, J. D. (2007). Mindfulness: Theoretical foundations and evidence for its salutary effects. *Psychological Inquiry,* 18(4), 211-237.

Bryant, F. & Veroff, J. (2007). Savoring: A new model of positive experience. Mahwah, NJ: Lawrence Erlbaum Associates.

Cacioppo, J.T., Gardner, W.L., & Bemtson, G.G. (1997). Beyond bipolar conceptualizations and measures: The case of attitudes and evaluative space. *Personality and Social Psychology Review,* 1, 3- 25.

Catalino, L. I., Algoe, S. B., & Fredrickson, B. L. (2014). Prioritizing positivity: An effective approach to pursuing happiness? *Emotion,* 14(6), 1155.

Clough, P., & Strycharczyk, D. (2012). *Developing Mental Toughness: Improving Performance, Wellbeing and Positive Behaviour in Others.* Kogan Page.

Crust, L. (2009). The relationship between mental toughness and affect intensity. *Personality and Individual Differences,* 47(8), 959–963. www.doi.org/10.1016/j.paid.2009.07.023

Crust, L., & Azadi, K. (2010). Mental toughness and athletes' use of psychological strategies. *European Journal of Sport Science,* 10(1), 43–51. www.doi.org/10.1080/17461390903049972

Crust, L., & Keegan, R. (2010). Mental toughness and attitudes to risk-taking. *Personality and Individual Differences,* 49(3), 164–168. www.doi.org/10.1016/j.paid.2010.03.026

da Silva, S. P., vanOyen Witvliet, C., & Riek, B. (2017). Self-forgiveness and forgiveness-seeking in response to rumination: Cardiac and emotional responses of transgressors. *The Journal of Positive Psychology,* 12(4), 362-372.

Danner, D. D., Snowdon, D. A., & Friesen, W. V. (2001). Positive emotions in early life and longevity: findings from the nun study. *Journal of Personality and Social Psychology,* 80(5), 804.

Deci, E. L., & Ryan, R. M. (2008). Self-determination theory: A macrotheory of human motivation, development, and health. *Canadian Psychology/ Psychologie Canadienne,* 49(3), 182.

Dewhurst, S. A., Anderson, R. J., Cotter, G., Crust, L., & Clough, P. J. (2012). Identifying the cognitive basis of mental toughness: Evidence from the directed forgetting paradigm. *Personality and Individual Differences,* 53(5), 587–590. www.doi.org/10.1016/j.paid.2012.04.036

Diener, E., Wirtz, D., Biswas-Diener, R., Tov, W., Kim-Prieto, C., Choi, D. W., & Oishi, S. (2009). New measures of well-being. In E. Diener (Ed.). *Assessing well-being* (pp. 247-266). Dordrecht, Netherlands: Springer Publishing Co.

Dweck, C. S. (2006). *Mindset: The new psychology of success.* New York, NY: Random House.

Ellis, A. (1957). Rational psychotherapy and individual psychology. *Journal of Individual Psychology,* 13(1), 38-44.

Ellis, A., & Dryden, W. (1987). *The practice of rational-emotive therapy (RET).* New York, NY: Springer Publishing Co.

Emmons, R. A. (1986). Personal strivings: An approach to personality and subjective well-being. *Journal of Personality and Social Psychology*, 51(5), 1058-1068.

Emmons, R., & McCullough, M. (2003). Counting blessings versus burdens. *Journal of Personality and Social Psychology,* 84(2), 377-389.

Fazio, R. H., Eiser, J. R., & Shook, N. J. (2004). Attitude formation through exploration: valence asymmetries. *Journal of Personality and Social Psychology,* 87, 293–311.

Finkenauer, C., & Rimé, B. (1998). Socially shared emotional experiences vs. emotional experiences kept secret: Differential characteristics and consequences. *Journal of Social and Clinical Psychology*, 17(3), 295-318.

Fredrickson, B. L. (1998). What good are positive emotions? *Review of General Psychology,* 2, 300-319.

Fredrickson, B. L. (2001). The role of positive emotions in positive psychology: The broaden-and-build theory of positive emotions. *American Psychologist,* 56, 218-226.

Fredrickson, B. L., & Losada, M. F. (2005). Positive affect and the complex dynamics of human flourishing. *American Psychologist,* 60(7), 678.

Flyvbjerg, B., Garbuio, M., & Lovallo, D. (2009). Delusion and deception in large infrastructure projects: two models for explaining and preventing executive disaster. *California management review,* 51(2), 170-194.

Gable, S. L., & Haidt, J. (2005). What (and why) is positive psychology? *Review of General Psychology,* 9, 103-110.

Gerber, M., Lang, C., Feldmeth, A. K., Elliot, C., Brand, S., Holsboer-Trachsler, E., & Pühse, U. (2013). Burnout and Mental Health in Swiss Vocational

Students: The Moderating Role of Physical Activity. *Journal of Research on Adolescence,* 25(1), 63–74. www.doi.org/10.1111/jora.12097

Govindji, R., & Linley, P. A. (2007). Strengths use, self-concordance and well-being: Implications for strengths coaching and coaching psychologists. *International Coaching Psychology Review,* 2(2), 143-153.

Grant, A. M., & Greene, J. (2001). *Coach Yourself: Make real change in your life.* London, England: Momentum Press.

Grant, A. M., Green, L. S., & Rynsaardt, J. (2010). Developmental coaching for high school teachers: Executive coaching goes to school. *Consulting Psychology Journal: Practice and Research,* 62(3), 151.

Grant, A. M., & Schwartz, B. (2011). Too much of a good thing: The challenge and opportunity of the inverted U. *Perspectives on Psychological Science,* 6(1), 61-76.

Green, L. S., Oades, L. G., & Grant, A. M. (2006). Cognitive-behavioural, solution focused life coaching: Enhancing goal striving, well-being and hope. *The Journal of Positive Psychology,* 1, 142-149.

Gucciardi, D. F., Gordon, S., & Dimmock, J. A. (2009). Evaluation of a Mental Toughness Training Program for Youth-Aged Australian Footballers: I. A Quantitative Analysis. *Journal of Applied Sport Psychology,* 21(3), 307–323. www.doi.org/10.1080/10413200903026066

Hayes, S. C., Strosahl, K., & Wilson, K. G. (1999). *Acceptance and Commitment Therapy: An experiential approach to behavior change.* New York, NY: Guilford Press.

Heifetz, R. A., Grashow, A., & Linsky, M. (2009). *The practice of adaptive leadership: Tools and tactics for changing your organization and the world.* Boston, MA; Harvard Business Press.

Hill, P. L., & Turiano, N. A. (2014). Purpose in life as a predictor of mortality across adulthood. *Psychological Science,* 25(7), 1482-1486.

Huppert, F.A. (2005). Positive mental health in individuals and populations. In F.A. Huppert, B. Keverne, & N. Baylis (Eds.), *The science of well-being* (pp. 307-340). Oxford, England: Oxford University Press.

Kabat-Zinn, J. (1990). *Full catastrophe living: Using the wisdom of your body and mind to face stress, pain and illness.* New York, NY: Delacorte.

Keyes, C. (2007). Promoting and protecting mental health as flourishing: A complementary strategy for improving national mental health. *American Psychologist,* 62, 95-108.

Linehan, M. M. (1993). *Skills training manual for treating borderline personality disorder.* New York, NY: Guilford Press.

Linley, A., Willars, J., & Biswas-Diener, R. (2010). *The strengths book: What you can do, love to do, and find it hard to do – and why it matters.* Coventry, England: CAPP Press.

Littman-Ovadia, H., & Russo-Netzer, P. (2018). Prioritizing positivity across the adult lifespan: initial evidence for differential associations with positive and negative emotions. *Quality of Life Research,* 28(2), 411-420.

Locke, E. A., & Latham, G. P. (2002). Building a practically useful theory of goal setting and task motivation: A 35-year odyssey. *American Psychologist,* 57(9), 705.

Lyubomirsky, S., Dickerhoof, R., Boehm, J. K., & Sheldon, K. M. (2011). Becoming happier takes both a will and a proper way: an experimental longitudinal intervention to boost well-being. *Emotion,* 11(2), 391.

Lyubomirsky, S., King, L., Diener, E. (2005) The benefits of frequent positive affect: Does happiness lead to success? *Psychological Bulletin,* 131(6), 803-855.

Marchant, D. C., Greig, M., & Scott, C. (2009). Attentional Focusing Instructions Influence Force Production and Muscular Activity During Isokinetic Elbow Flexions. *Journal of Strength and Conditioning Research,* 23(8), 2358–2366. www.doi.org/10.1519/jsc.0b013e3181b8d1e5

Markus, H., & Nurius, P. (1986). Possible selves. *American Psychologist,* 41(9), 954.

Martínez-Martí, M. L., & Ruch, W. (2014). Character strengths and well-being across the life span: data from a representative sample of German-speaking adults living in Switzerland. *Frontiers in Psychology,* 5, 1253.

Mattie, P., & Munroe-Chandler, K. (2012). Examining the Relationship Between Mental Toughness and Imagery Use. *Journal of Applied Sport Psychology,* 24(2), 144–156. www.doi.org/10.1080/10413200.2011.605422

McCullough, M. E., Kilpatrick, S. D., Emmons, R. A., & Larson, D. B. (2001). Is gratitude a moral affect? *Psychological Bulletin,* 127(2), 249.

McGrath, R. E. (2015). Integrating psychological and cultural perspectives on virtue: The hierarchical structure of character strengths. *The Journal of Positive Psychology,* 10(5), 407-424.

Moradi, J., Mousavi, M. V., & Amirtash, A. M. (2013). The role of mental toughness in acquisition and retention of a sports skill. *European Journal of Experimental Biology,* 3(6).

Muraven, M., & Baumeister, R. F. (2000). Self-regulation and depletion of limited resources: Does self-control resemble a muscle? *Psychological Bulletin,* 126(2), 247.

Muraven, M., & Slessareva, E. (2003). Mechanisms of self-control failure: Motivation and limited resources. *Personality and Social Psychology Bulletin*, 29(7), 894–906.

Nicholls, A. R., Polman, R. C. J., & Levy, A. R. (2012). A path analysis of stress appraisals, emotions, coping, and performance satisfaction among athletes. *Psychology of Sport and Exercise,* 13(3), 263–270. www.doi.org/10.1016/j.psychsport.2011.12.003

Nicholls, A. R., Polman, R. C. J., Levy, A. R., & Backhouse, S. H. (2008). Mental toughness, optimism, pessimism, and coping among athletes. *Personality and Individual Differences,* 44(5), 1182–1192. www.doi.org/10.1016/j.paid.2007.11.011

Niemiec, R. (2014). *Mindfulness and character strengths: A practical guide to flourishing.* Göttingen, Germany: Hogrefe Publishing Group.

Norem, J. K., & Chang, E. C. (2002). The positive psychology of negative thinking. *Journal of Clinical Psychology,* 58(9), 993-1001.

Nussbaum, A. D., & Dweck, C. S. (2008). Defensiveness Versus Remediation: Self-Theories and Modes of Self-Esteem Maintenance. *Personality and Social Psychology Bulletin,* 34(5), 599–612. www.doi.org/10.1177/0146167207312960

Oettingen, G. (1996). Positive fantasy and motivation. In P. M. Gollwitzer & J. A. Bargh (Eds.), *The psychology of action: Linking cognition and motivation to behavior* (pp. 236-259). New York, NY: Guilford Press.

Park, N., Peterson, C., & Seligman, M. E. (2004). Strengths of character and well-being. *Journal of Social and Clinical Psychology,* 23(5), 603-619.

Park, N., Peterson, C., & Seligman, M. E. (2006). Character strengths in fifty-four nations and the fifty US states. *The Journal of Positive Psychology,* 1(3), 118-129.

Peterson, C., Park, N., & Seligman, M. E. P. (2005). Orientations to happiness and life satisfaction: The full life versus the empty life. *Journal of Happiness Studies, 6*(1), 25-41.

Peterson, C., & Seligman, M. E. P. (2004). *Character strengths and virtues: A handbook and classification.* New York, NY & Washington, D.C.: Oxford University Press & American Psychological Association.

Peterson, C., & Steen, T. A. (2009). Optimistic explanatory style. In S. J. Lopez & C. R. Snyder (Eds.), Oxford library of psychology. *Oxford handbook of positive psychology* (pp. 313-321). New York, NY: Oxford University Press.

Prochaska, J. & DiClemente, C. (1983) Stages and processes of self-change in smoking: Toward an integrative model of change. *Journal of Consulting and Clinical Psychology, 51*(3), 390-395.

Proyer, R. T., Gander, F., Wellenzohn, S., & Ruch, W. (2015). Strengths-based positive psychology interventions: A randomized placebo-controlled online trial on long-term effects for a signature strengths- vs. a lesser strengths-intervention. *Frontiers in Psychology, 6*, 456.

Ricard, M. (2015). *Happiness: A guide to developing life's most important skill.* London, England: Atlantic Books Ltd.

Rozin, P., & Royzman, E. B. (2001). Negativity bias, negativity dominance, and contagion. *Personality and Social Psychology Review, 5*(4), 296-320.

Rusk, R. D., & Waters, L. E. (2013). Tracing the size, reach, impact, and breadth of positive psychology. *The Journal of Positive Psychology, 8*(3), 207-221.

Scharmer, C. O., & Kaufer, K. (2013). *Leading from the emerging future: From ego-system to eco-system economies.* San Francisco, CA: Berrett-Koehler Publishers.

Schutte, N. S., & Malouff, J. M. (2019). The impact of signature character strengths interventions: A meta-analysis. *Journal of Happiness Studies,* 20(4), 1179-1196.

Seligman, M. E. P., Steen, T., Park, N., & Peterson, C. (2005). *Positive psychology progress: Empirical validation of interventions.* American Psychologist, 60(5), 410-421.

Seligman, M. E. (2002). Positive psychology, positive prevention, and positive therapy. In C. Snyder & S. Lopez (Eds.), *Handbook of positive psychology* (pp. 3-12). New York, NY: Oxford University Press.

Sheldon, K. M., & Elliot, A. J. (1999). Goal striving, need satisfaction, and longitudinal well-being: The self-concordance model. *Journal of Personality and Social Psychology,* 76(3), 482.

Sheldon, K. M., Kasser, T., Smith, K., & Share, T. (2002). Personal goals and psychological growth: Testing an intervention to enhance goal attainment and personality integration. *Journal of Personality,* 70(1), 5-31.

Sheldon, K. M., & Krieger, L. S. (2014). Walking the talk: Value importance, value enactment, and well-being. *Motivation and Emotion,* 38(5), 609-619.

Sheldon, K. M., & Lyubomirsky, S. (2006). How to increase and sustain positive emotion: The effects of expressing gratitude and visualizing best possible selves. *The Journal of Positive Psychology,* 1(2), 73-82.

Slemp, G. R., & Vella-Brodrick, D. A. (2013). The job crafting questionnaire: A new scale to measure the extent to which employees engage in job crafting. *International Journal of Wellbeing,* 3(2).

Smith, J. L., & Hanni, A. A. (2017). Effects of a savoring intervention on resilience and well-being of older adults. *Journal of Applied Gerontology,* 38(1), 137-152.

Smyth, J. M. (1998). Written emotional expression: Effect sizes, outcome types, and moderating variables. *Journal of Consulting and Clinical Psychology,* 66(1), 174.

Snyder, C. R. (2002). Hope theory: Rainbows in the mind. *Psychological Inquiry,* 13(4), 249-275.

Snyder, C. R., Michael, S. T., & Cheavens, J. S. (1999). Hope as a psychotherapeutic foundation of common factors, placebos, and expectancies. In M. A. Hubble, B. L. Duncan, & S. D. Miller (Eds.), *The heart and soul of change: What works in therapy* (pp. 179-200). Washington, D.C.: American Psychological Association.

Snyder, C. R., Sympson, S. C., Ybasco, F. C., Borders, T. F., Babyak, M. A., & Higgins, R. L. (1996). Development and validation of the State Hope Scale. *Journal of Personality and Social Psychology,* 2, 321-335.

Spaten, O. M., & Green, S. (2018). Delivering value in coaching through exploring meaning, purpose, values, and strengths. In J. Passmore, B. Underhill, & M. Goldsmith (Eds.), *Mastering executive coaching* (pp. 90-110). New York, NY: Routledge.

Sparks, J., & Ledgerwood, A. (2017). When good is stickier than bad: Understanding gain/loss asymmetries in sequential framing effects. *Journal of Experimental Psychology: General,* 146(8), 1086-1105.

St Clair-Thompson, H., Bugler, M., Robinson, J., Clough, P., McGeown, S. P., & Perry, J. (2014). Mental toughness in education: exploring relationships with attainment, attendance, behaviour and peer relationships. *Educational Psychology,* 35(7), 886–907. www.doi.org/10.1080/01443410.2014.895294

Steger, M. F. (2017). Creating meaning and purpose at work. In L. G. Oades, M. F. Steger, A. Delle Fave, & J. Passmore (Eds.), Wiley Blackwell handbook of the psychology of positivity and strengths-based approaches at work (pp.

60–81). Hoboken, NJ: John Wiley & Sons.

Swann Jr, W. B., & Schroeder, D. G. (1995). The search for beauty and truth: A framework for understanding reactions to evaluations. *Personality and Social Psychology Bulletin*, 21(12), 1307-1318.

Tolstoy L. (1918). The three questions. In: Tolstoy L. *What Men Live By and Other Tales.* Boston, MA: The Stratford Company.

Wagner, L., Gander, F., Proyer, R. T., & Ruch, W. (2019). Character strengths and PERMA: Investigating the relationships of character strengths with a multidimensional framework of well-being. *Applied Research in Quality of Life,* 1-22.

Wood, J. V., Perunovic, W. Q. E., & Lee, J. W. (2009). Positive self-statements: Power for some, peril for others. *Psychological Science,* 20(7), 860-866.

Worthington, E. (2008). *Steps to REACH forgiveness and to reconcile.* Boston, MA: Pearson Custom Publishing.

Wrzesniewski, A., McCauley, C., Rozin, P., & Schwartz, B. (1997). Jobs, careers, and callings: People's relations to their work. *Journal of Research in Personality,* 31(1), 21-33.

Young, K. C., Kashdan, T. B., & Macatee, R. (2015). Strength balance and implicit strength measurement: New considerations for research on strengths of character. *The Journal of Positive Psychology,* 10(1), 17-24.

www.ingramcontent.com/pod-product-compliance
Lightning Source LLC
Chambersburg PA
CBHW041256040426
42334CB00028BA/3032